Longman Practice Exams

for the

Cambridge Certificate in Advanced English

Roy Kingsbury   Felicity O'Dell   Guy Wellman

Longman

Longman Group UK Ltd.
Longman House, Burnt Mill, Harlow,
Essex CM20 2JE, England
and Associated Companies throughout
the world.

First published 1991
Third impression 1992

ISBN 0 582 01809 9

Set in 12/14pt ITC Garamond Light and 10/11pt Frutiger Roman, Adobe (postscript)

Printed in Hong Kong
WC/03

Acknowledgements

We are grateful to the following for permission to reproduce copyright material:
American Express Holidays for an extract from 'Take a Break' *Short Break Holidays in Europe* brochure April 89 – March 90; Facts of Living Publications for an extract from a *Facts of Living Survey;* Guardian News Service Ltd for extracts from articles 'The all-American way of education...' (abridged) by Sylvia Hall & 'Still-life study, with bleeps' by Maev Kennedy in *The Guardian* 4.1.90 & 5.1.90; The Green Magazine Co Ltd for extracts from the article 'Basket Cases' in *Green Magazine* January 90; Hamfield Publications Ltd for an abridged extract from the article 'What a day for the bailiff' by Martin Plimmer in *Plus* Magazine 20.12.89; the Controller of Her Majesty's Stationery Office for an abridged extract from *Practical Ways to Crack Crime* (2nd edition, 1989) issued for the Home Office for the Central Office of Information; Hodder & Stoughton Ltd/Madison Publishing for an abridged extract from *The Discovery of the Titanic* by Dr Robert Ballard; IPC Women's Magazines Group for the abridged article 'Four's a crowd' by Jackie Robb from *Me* Magazine 22.6.89; Maclean Hunter for an extract and map from the article 'The Danube River Blues' by Mary McIver from Maclean's 11.1.88; the Author Bryan Magee & his agents for an extract from his article 'Women's Rights and Wrongs' in *The Weekend Guardian* 11-12.11.89; The Observer Ltd for an extract from the article 'When testing can become a tyranny' by Ted Wragg & the article; 'It's there in cold print' by Martin Bailey in *The Observer* 30.7.89 & 23.7.89; Patey Doyle Ltd for an extract from the article 'Planning Ahead' by Ellen Knudsen in *The Office Magazine* 9.86; Penguin Books Ltd for an adapted extract from *Who Cares About English Usage?* by David Crystal, copyright © David Crystal 1984; Random Century Group for an extract from 'The Creative Leap' in *The Visible Persuaders* by Denis Thomas, publ. Hutchinsons, © Denis Thomas 1967; the Author, Anne Thwaite for her article 'Grim Tales' in *The Guardian* 28.9.89; Time Out Magazine Ltd for 'Theatre ads' in *Time Out* 27.6.90-4.7.90; Times Newspapers Ltd for extracts from the articles 'Photographing Sport' by David Brittain in *Manual of Creative Photography,* 'Walking' by Prof. Peter Fentem in *A–Z of Preventive Medicine* & 'An Old Man's Pride' by Brian Jackman in the *Sunday Times Magazine* 14.5.89, 5.11.89 & 1.10.89. © Times Newspapers Ltd 1989; Toyota (GB) Ltd & the Author, Jeffrey Zollo for an extract from his article 'Spycatchers' in *Toyota Today* Magazine, June '89; World Publications Ltd for an abridged extract from the article 'White Death' in *World* Magazine, Feb. '89.

'Superbrats' strike back

I AM a 15-year-old girl who, judging by the advertising agency's report you quoted, is an abuser of the environment, alcoholic, money-mad and sex-crazed (page A3, last week). I don't know who the agency interviewed, but that's not the way I see *my* generation growing up.

This letter is written on recycled paper. I am also a strict vegetarian, as is my 12-year-old brother. At school, I have given a talk on water pollution, done a topic on world conflict and learned about illegal whaling in the Antarctic.

It is your generation that bore us and brought us up and taught us all we know; all we needed to do was to put things into perspective and make up our own minds. We are not the uncaring generation you have made us out to be.

Claire Craig
Chinnor, Oxford

EXAGGERATED: As a 15-year-old, I feel the report on our moral standards is exaggerated. Teenagers are more aware of Aids and of environmental issues than our elders think we are capable of.

Surely if a 15-year-old wrote an article headlined "Enter super-ageds, the geriatrics of the 1990s", it would be unrepresentative if it was only based on such a report. Is there really such a lack of faith in the young?

Lucy van Beek
Rotherfield, East Sussex

UNFAIR: How disheartening to return from taking my 15-year-old son to hockey practice to read that he would rather be lying on the floor holding a can of lager and watching EastEnders.

The adman's image of the superbrats of the 1990s is different from my experience during the past week, when I have discussed with my son the problems of designing a new toy for three-year-olds, the reasons why the distribution of lichen may vary between Tynemouth and Cornwall and the importance of considering other people's feelings in group social activities.

Is the North-South divide so great that we have a different type of 15-year-old here, or are we being presented with yet another figment of the adman's imagination? Of course our children watch television and have aspirations for the future, but the programme is more likely to be the Super Bowl playoffs than EastEnders, and the aspiration to have a better environment rather than a faster car.

David Parker
Gosforth, Newcastle

ADMAN'S DREAM: This idea of the 1990s being a decade of unrestrained romper-room consumerism at the expense of helpless parents smacks of the adman's dream. I predict that with advances in technology and the continual trimming of workforces, this "demographic time-bomb" will be a damp squib.

It is wrong for anybody to suggest that children will "hardly have to lift a finger" when it comes to finding a job, bearing in mind that these supposed superbrats "cherish ambitions to earn pots of money". You don't just "pick up" a degree, especially if you're a lager-swilling couch potato whose interests don't extend beyond pubescent sex and EastEnders.

T Smith
Tunley, Gloucestershire

UNREPRESENTATIVE: I can't help wondering about the validity of this research, based as it was on a survey of just 327 children. Certainly, the picture painted is not one I recognise when I look at the students I teach and my teenage children's friends.

Adrian Starr
Whitley Bay, Tyne & Wear

'EastEnders': a popular British TV 'soap opera'
Tynemouth: a fishing port on the north bank of the Tyne River in the north-east of England
Cornwall: the county in the far south-west corner of the British Isles
the Super Bowl: the final (championship) game at the end of the professional American football season
Jekyll and Hyde Jr.: a 'junior' version of the main character in Robert Louis Stevenson's novel *Dr Jekyll and Mr Hyde*, who has a dual personality, good and evil

2 Questions 16–19. Read this extract from a book and answer the multiple-choice questions. You must choose the answer or sentence completion which you think fits best — **A, B, C** or **D**. Give **one answer only** to each question.

The Future of the Wreck of the *Titanic* –Sanctuary or Salvage?

As long as the wreck is left unmolested by treasure-hunters, the *Titanic* won't appear to change much in my lifetime. The prevailing currents, which gave us so much trouble on some dives, will continue to build up a sediment around the 'windward' sides of the large pieces of wreckage, but complete burial under sediments falling from above would take less than a thousand years for the smaller pieces, nearly one million years for the two large hull sections. Before then, iron-eating bacteria would have finished their demolition work. The build-up of sediment this far out in the ocean is very slow and even the smallest objects we saw, such as the doll's head, showed very little evidence of burial despite the passage of 75 years. Since the ship sits in an area of underwater sand dunes, the surrounding terrain will shift as the dunes migrate, revealing currently buried pieces of debris and covering up things we saw.

In the longer term, the rust-forming bacteria will continue to do their work. Gradually, the ship will be eaten away until its remaining structural integrity is threatened. My colleague Holger Jannasch predicts that in another 75 years, perhaps a little longer, the R.M.S. *Titanic* will most likely be a jumble of rubble, its noble bow section only a memory. Certain things will still be there to see — mostly in the debris field: ceramic, bronze, and brass remains; lumps of coal. But it will not be a pretty sight.

For now, the greatest threat to the *Titanic* clearly comes from man, particularly in the form of crude dredging operations. There are all sorts of fishing boats and drill ships that could be hired to go out to the site and attempt to bring up pieces of wreckage. But most artifacts of any value lie scattered in the debris field and would have to be salvaged by a sub with a mechanical arm.

The legislation passed by the United States Congress and signed into law by the President, calling for the wreck to be made an international memorial and left unmolested, should discourage most treasure-seekers. At least it guarantees them bad publicity. My simple wish is that any who do mount new expeditions to visit the wreck will respect the site as I have.

16 What is likely to do the most damage to the wreck over the next few years?

A Sediment.
B Treasure-hunters.
C Shifting sand.
D Iron-eating bacteria.

17 Experts believe that in another 75 years all that will be left of the ship will be

A the major front section.
B an outline structure.
C small pieces of debris.
D a mass of bits and pieces.

18 Any salvage operation would be difficult because people would need

A a submarine.
B a drilling ship.
C sand-digging equipment.
D a dredger.

19 The writer seems to be very worried that other people may

A be put off attempting salvage.
B reach the wreck before him.
C damage articles they might find.
D not treat the wreck with respect.

3 Questions 20–29. In the following piece, giving tips on how people, and women in particular, can protect themselves, the sub-headings (20–29) have been taken out and listed below (**A–M**). Write the appropriate letter (**A–M**) beside each number (20–29). Three of the headings listed below do not belong in the piece.

If you are a man, don't stop reading or turn the page. Although this information is mainly for women, you should be aware of it too. The best way to minimise the risk of attack is by taking these precautions:

20 ....Check and, if necessary, strengthen the security of your house or flat. Draw your curtains after dark to discourage any Peeping Tom. If you think there is a prowler outside, don't go out to check — dial 999.

21 ....Use only your surname and initials in the telephone directory and on the doorplate if you live in a flat. That way, a stranger cannot tell whether a man or woman lives there.

22 ....When moving into a new home it makes sense to change the front and back door locks — other people may have keys that fit. *Never* forget to use the locks! If you are selling your home, try not to show people around on your own. Ask your estate agent to send a representative with prospective buyers.

23 ....Avoid short-cuts through dimly-lit alleys or across waste ground. Walk facing the traffic so a car cannot pull up behind you unnoticed. Walk on the street side of the pavement, so an attacker lurking in an alley has further to come to reach you.

24 ....If you regularly walk home after dark, consider buying a screech alarm, available from the security department of many DIY shops.

25 ....If you're going to be out late, try to arrange a lift home or book a taxi. When you get home, ask the driver to wait until you are inside.

26 ....Particularly after dark, try to avoid using isolated bus stops. On a bus, sit near the driver or conductor. On a train, sit in a compartment where there are several other people — ideally in a compartment which will be near the exit at your destination.

27 ....Before going on any long journey, make sure your vehicle is in good condition. Plan your route in advance, using main roads as far as possible, and have enough money and petrol.

28 ....If somebody flags you down on a quiet road, make sure it is a genuine emergency before you open a window or get out of the car. If you are in any doubt, go on and call the police.

29 ....It is sensible to think about what you would be prepared to do if you were physically attacked. Could you fight back or would you play along and wait for a chance to escape? Preparing yourself for all possibilities could provide a split-second advantage.

A OUT ON FOOT
B WHEN DRIVING
C WHEN AT HOME
D ON PUBLIC TRANSPORT
E ACCEPTING LIFTS
F IF THE WORST HAPPENS
G GETTING HOME IN THE EARLY HOURS
H BE WARY OF HITCHHIKERS
I NEVER WALK ANYWHERE
J ON THE MOVE?-MAKE A FRESH START
K YOUR OWN PORTABLE SECURITY KIT
L DON'T SPELL OUT WHAT THEY WANT TO KNOW
M IF YOU HAVE BEEN ATTACKED

Pedal power v Porsche

What's the quickest way to get to work through town traffic each day - car or bike? And who gets more hot and bothered?

1 The race between the two Carreras started on the long incline that feeds south London commuter traffic into Blackheath's congested High Street. The driver in the 150 mph Porsche Carrera inched forward in the familiar snake of cars, a cellular phone ready to hand in case he felt in danger of missing a business appointment, *writes Daniel Ward.*

My Carrera crept past him... despite relying on pedal power. My vehicle is the latest in all-terrain bicycles, a super smart Carrera machine which scores on street credibility with its high-tech looks. Knobbly tyres, rugged chrome alloy frame, quick-release everything and 18 gears make the grey and yellow machine the Range Rover of the bike world.

2 The Porsche stayed behind for a couple of miles, even as I struggled against the blustery conditions across Blackheath. I had learned that rapid flicking between gears was the best way to keep up the momentum as the legs begin to weaken.

Thirty-five minutes of cycling to evaluate the merits of travelling to work on two wheels rather than four was hot and hard - and I had yet to reach the halfway point in the 11-mile journey that can take an hour of bumper-to-bumper crawl in a car.

3 The steep hill down to Deptford brought some relief, but the Porsche went past. However, my advantage was still to come - a mile-long dawdle close to the Thames where the buses-only lane brings daily congestion. As the traffic piled up, the bike came into its own and I stopped thinking about my flagging pedal power. It was another three miles before the Porsche swept by for the last time.

4 Bus lanes are great for cyclists, apart from the noxious clouds of black smoke buses emit as they start off. And I discovered that not only is cycling tiring but that in London it can be a filthy business. In Rotherhithe tunnel the exhaust fumes were less noticeable than the dust and litter swirling around.

5 I also found having 18 gears on a bike was as unnecessary as a Porsche driver in a jam having 150 mph potential under his foot.

Psychologically, it seems that we like to know our machines are capable of much more than is required of them.

The all-terrain bike, which originated in California, is at least highly practical, proving vastly easier on its rider in town than a racing bike. Big tyres soak up the worst of the bumps and the rugged frame does not flinch at the pot-holes. The brakes seem more powerful than on a racer and the straight handlebars are sensible

I arrived at work, hot and grimy, a respectable five minutes later than I would have done by car. So with practice a cycle could match the pace of a car. Unfortunately, I still have to find the energy to slog back home.

Carrera prices: a Porsche costs around £40,000. Halford's two-wheeler £299.

4 Questions 30–38. Read the article carefully. Which points did the writer Daniel Ward make? Tick (√) if you think he did. Put a dash '—' if you don't think he made the point.

30 At the start of the race both Carreras moved slowly in the traffic. 30 ...

31 The writer carried a portable telephone with him in case he had to ring the office. 31 ...

32 The bicycle was both elegant and powerfully built. 32 ...

33 It only took the writer 35 minutes to get halfway to work. 33 ...

34 Traffic is often congested in London because of special bus lanes. 34 ...

35 The writer overtook the car on the road near the Thames. 35 ...

36 All in all, cycling to work in London is a dirty experience. 36 ...

37 When cycling into London it's an advantage to have a large number of gears on your bicycle. 37 ...

38 The state of the roads made cycling difficult for the writer. 38 ...

Questions 39–43. The following questions ask you to choose the correct or most appropriate heading for each section numbered **1–5** in the text opposite. **A–H** below list possible section headings. Match the correct or most appropriate headings from **A–H** to the sections **1–5**.

NOTE: There is **only one answer** to each question.

Possible section headings

39 ...Section **1**

40 ...Section **2**

41 ...Section **3**

42 ...Section **4**

43 ...Section **5**

A The Porsche wins

B Struggling to halfway

C Hot and bothered

D Unclean

E More technology than necessary

F They're away!

G The bus lane's the fast lane

H Pedal power wins by a mile

PAPER 2: WRITING

Time: 2 hours

Section A

Read the advertisement opposite about job-sharing. You are very interested in doing work on this basis. You ring Naomi to find out more about the scheme. You make the notes which you can see below while you are speaking to her.

After making the phone-call, you decide to write to a friend who used to do the same kind of work as you. Your friend would like to work, but has circumstances which make it impossible for him or her to work full-time. Explain why you think it would be convenient for you and your friend to share a job between you. Suggest how you could organise your work and ask for your friend's comments. Also make a proposal to your friend as to what should be your next step to try to get yourselves employed by the Council as job-sharers.

Read the advertisement (opposite) and the notes (below) carefully and then write the letter to your friend. You should write approximately 250 words.

Kinds of jobs sharing suitable for — teachers of all kinds — all kinds of office workers — librarians — gardeners — all sorts of medical staff — mechanics — builders and maintenance workers — social workers of all kinds — police, traffic wardens, garage attendants

Better chance if I apply w. partner.

Job-sharers need to — communicate well w. each other, be esp. conscientious, be prepared to co-operate rather than compete w. each other, be reasonably flexible and tolerant

Council needs to know
what kind of work we'd be interested in (in general, details not necessary) — our work experience and qualifs. — how we'd like to divide our hrs. — if we see job-sharing as perm. or just temp. arrangement — why we feel we cd. work well tog.

Write to: Ms Naomi Hannay,
Personnel Department,
City of Cambridge Council,
Shire Hall,
Cambridge CB5 4BF

City of Cambridge

Finding it difficult to balance the demands of home and a full-time job?

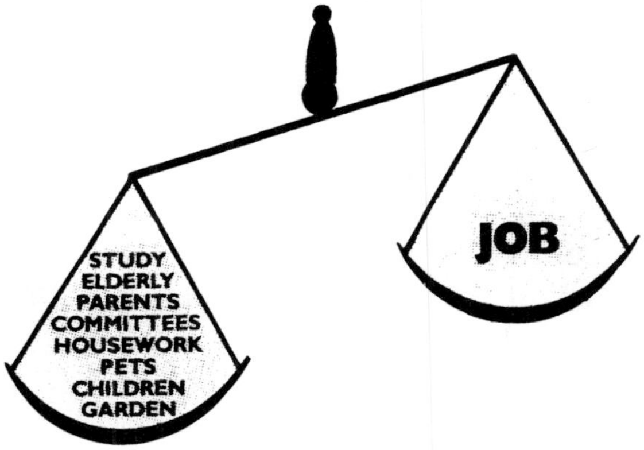

HAVE YOU THOUGHT OF JOB SHARING?

Job sharing is when two people share a full-time job. Each person does part of the job and receives a proportional part of the wages and benefits according to the hours worked.

It is particularly suitable for people who cannot or do not want to work full-time because of:

- *caring for young children*
- *caring for other dependant relatives*
- *part-time studying*
- *disability or illness*
- *serving on public bodies*

Most of the Council's 1,200 jobs are open to job sharers. Whenever a new job or vacancy is advertised, unless it specifically says otherwise in the advertisement, we are pleased to receive applications from either a pair of job sharers or someone looking for a partner to share a job.

We now have a job share register and can help put job sharers in touch with a partner interested in doing similar work.

To join our job share register or to find out more about employment opportunities with the City Council, please telephone Naomi or Margaret in Personnel on (0223) 463235 for an application form and/or a copy of our Vacancy Bulletin.

Our attractive benefits package includes child care subsidy, matrnity and paternity leave, flexible working hours and a subsidised Staff Restaurant.

We are working for equal opportunity in employment and service provision and positively welcome applicants from all sections of the community.

Working for the Community!

Section B

Choose ONE of the following writing tasks. Your answer should follow exactly the instructions given. You are advised to write approximately 250 words.

1 A project is being undertaken to construct a large new building in your neighbourhood, and the authorities are going to bury a 'Time capsule' under the foundations. (A 'Time capsule' is a box containing a variety of objects, including videos, photographs, writings and music, which will together give people in the distant future an idea of life today.) One thing the authorities want to include is a collection of thoughts and impressions from twenty young people about life today in your neighbourhood. They have set up a competition to make a selection.
Write your entry for this competition.

2 Your town or home area is keen to host a major international conference in a couple of years' time, but the organisers are not sure that it is a suitable venue. They are concerned that there will not be enough for spouses and children accompanying delegates to do during the day or for anyone to do in the evenings.
Write a report to the organisers strongly defending the suitability of your town or area, and suggesting any special events or excursions that you feel should be organised.

3 You and your family have recently returned from a holiday in Canada. You think you left a number of things behind in the hotel where you were staying. **Write a letter** to the hotel giving any basic details of your stay that would be necessary to help them deal with your problem. Also provide a precise description of what you think you left there, explaining where you think you may have left the things and asking for them to be sent on to you. Don't forget to apologise for any inconvenience caused and to make some suggestion concerning payment of postage.

4 You have been asked to contribute a short article for a book in English for learners of English. The editors would like you to write about your experiences when you started learning the language. They would like you to write something that would help and/or amuse other students of English.
Write the article.

PAPER 3: ENGLISH IN USE

Time: 1 hour 30 minutes

Section A

1 Complete the following article by writing the missing words in the spaces provided. Use **only one word** in each space. The first one has been done for you as an example.

The Power of Garlic

My husband's favourite cookery book is *The Garlic Book*. It contains recipes for ..*such*... (1) unusual things as garlic sweets, garlic drinks and garlic ice-cream. He believes — .... (2) do a number of modern researchers — that garlic has all sorts of medicinal properties. It has now been proved that it not .... (3) acts as an antiseptic but also reduces the risk .... (4) heart disease. For example, a recently published investigation shows that in southern European countries, ... (5) garlic eating is common, heart attacks occur .... (6) frequently than in the north. Another study shows that .... (7) garlic is taken daily, the cholesterol level of the average person is lowered .... (8) 10 to 15 per cent.

Garlic is believed to .... (9) originated in the Siberian desert and, up until the middle of the 18th century, Siberians .... (10) their taxes in garlic — fifteen bulbs for a man, ten for a woman and five for a child. In ancient Egypt seven kilos .... (11) buy a slave.

.... (12) the world garlic has also from ancient times been considered to have magical powers, protecting people .... (13) vampires and other evils.

But .... (14) good for the health garlic may be, its use has always been limited .... (15) its tendency to make both breath and skin smell. Yet it is claimed that this problem .... (16) be solved by eating salads, and especially parsley, at the same time.

2 Read the article below and, in the items opposite, circle the letter next to the word which best fits each space. The first answer has been given as an example.

THE FIRST ALL-FEMALE CREW IN A 'ROUND THE WORLD RACE'

The Whitbread Round the World Race is one of the greatest and most dangerous journeys on (17) .... It is a sea voyage of 33,000 miles, and people from many countries (18) .... its progress with considerable interest. After all, for many, not least of which the sponsors of the different yachts, a great deal of money and prestige are (19) ....

One of the special features of the 1989/90 Race, however, was the entry of the yacht *Maiden Great Britain* with an all-female crew. The captain of the yacht was 26-year-old Tracy Edwards who (20) .... a long time planning for the challenge. It was after she had (21) .... part in the 1985/86 Race that she decided to form an all-female crew.

In order to assemble the crew she advertised (22) .... Among the original 460 applicants, there was even interest from countries as far (23) .... as China and Brazil. She then interviewed something in the (24) .... of 80 or 90 applicants, and managed to whittle the number down to the final international crew (25) .... 15 women — 13 on board and two on shore. The women came not only from Britain, but from France, Holland and New Zealand too.

(26) .... money to mount the challenge was extremely difficult. Not only were British companies reluctant to sponsor the project, Tracy also came up against sexual (27) .... It seemed that people just did not want to sponsor a yacht, however good, with an all-female crew. In the (28) ...., it was the Royal Jordanian Airlines that (29) .... their support — support which was reckoned to be about £1.5 million.

Although they had plenty of experience, none of the women except Tracy had ever (30) .... in a Whitbread Race before. For them it was a great challenge, and unknown (31) .... But one thing did give them a foretaste of the Round the World Race, and that was (32) .... in the Route of Discovery Race in December 1988 — a 3,800-mile race from Cadiz to the Dominican Republic.

17	**A** world	**B** sea	**C** earth	**D** yacht
18	**A** follow	**B** go after	**C** pursue	**D** wait for
19	**A** combined	**B** attached	**C** involved	**D** added
20	**A** passed	**B** took	**C** wanted	**D** spent
21	**A** taken	**B** done	**C** made	**D** had
22	**A** widely	**B** broadly	**C** greatly	**D** extremely
23	**A** way	**B** abroad	**C** distant	**D** afield
24	**A** number	**B** region	**C** area	**D** total
25	**A** making	**B** comprising	**C** adding	**D** consisting
26	**A** Pulling	**B** Raising	**C** Earning	**D** Piling
27	**A** argument	**B** reserve	**C** pride	**D** prejudice
28	**A** end	**B** final	**C** eventual	**D** last
29	**A** financed	**B** came to	**C** backed	**D** offered
30	**A** gone	**B** sailed	**C** done	**D** entered
31	**A** oceans	**B** area	**C** seas	**D** territory
32	**A** participating	**B** taking	**C** parting	**D** yachting

Section B

3 Read the following text carefully. In many lines, **although not all** , there is an extra and unnecessary word.

Put a line through each unnecessary word that you find and then write the word in the space provided at the end of the line. Some lines are correct. Indicate these lines with a tick (√) in the space provided. The first line has been done as an example.

You never know what it might be worth

The English seem to have a passion for ~~the~~ collecting. For	(33)...*the*....
centuries, they have been acquired, catalogued and stored things.	(34)..........
Men have actually made a name in the past as 'great collectors',	(35)..........
but nevertheless such single-minded pursuits were usually only	(36)..........
for the rich people.	(37)..........
Nowadays, it would seems, just about everyone collects	(38)..........
something — old 'Rock 'n' Roll' records, antique spoons, stamps,	(39)..........
postcards, some candlesticks, 19th-century kitchen utensils.	(40)..........
The list is endless — but because so many of people are looking	(41)..........
for items to add up to their collection, prices for the rarest, but	(42) ....
often the most ordinary-looking items, can be very high cost.	(43) ....
Take the children's books from early this century. Who would	(44) ....
have thought of that a first edition of J.R.R. Tolkien's book	(45) ....
The Hobbit , which it can't have cost much more than £2-£3	(46) ....
pounds when it was published in 1937, would now be worth	(47) ....
£5,000-£6,000?! Although to fetch that price, it must be said, a	(48) ....
copy has to be in perfect condition. But you'd expect that,	
wouldn't you?	

4 The language in the following draft of part of an advertisement for fitted bathrooms was considered far too formal by the manager to engage readers' interest. He has underlined and numbered parts which need simplifying.

Complete the numbered blanks in the improved final version at the bottom of the page **using not more than three words in each gap**. The first blank has been completed for you as an example.

There is no reason for you to [49] despair. Every inch of space in your bathroom will be expertly utilised [50]. There is not one [51] corner which cannot be beautifully transformed by Dolphin [52]. The reason is that [53] we offer the client a complete fitted bathroom service which is totally professional from commencement to completion [54]. We assist you in designing [55] the bathroom that you want. We assist you in selecting [56] the right suite, colours and accessories from the attractive range which you will find in the pages of [57] our fitted bathroom brochure. Further, it will be installed [58] for you to the last detail [59]. The implication of this is that [60] our installation experts are at your service to undertake [61] all the plumbing, wiring, plastering and tiling. We even lay the carpet. There will be no need for you [62] to do anything at all! [63]

(49) ..*Don't*... despair! We're (50) .... using every inch of space in your bathroom.

There (51) .... corner that Dolphin can't (52) ....

That's (53) .... we offer you a complete fitted bathroom service that's totally professional from (54) .... end.

We (55) .... design the bathroom you want. We (56) .... the right suite, colours and accessories from the attractive range (57) .... our fitted bathroom brochure. And (58) .... it for you from top to (59) ....

(60) .... our installation experts are at your service (61) .... all the plumbing, wiring, plastering and tiling. We even lay the carpet. You (62) .... to (63) .... a finger!

Section C

5 Choose the best phrases or sentences from those given opposite to fill the blanks in this text. Write one letter (**A–J**) in each of the numbered spaces.

NOTE: Five of the suggested phrases or sentences **do not fit at all.**

The Danube River blues

The notion of the picturesque Danube River, inspiration for Johann Strauss Jr.'s romantic *Blue Danube* waltz, reduced to a mere trickle is as unthinkable as the idea of Niagara Falls drying up. But that will be the result for at least part of the storied European waterway (64) ......J.................. , with the co-operation of neighbouring Austria. Work has begun on diverting a 120-mile portion of the Danube along the Hungarian-Czech border to generate electricity. (65) ....G.............. the project will despoil an ecologically unique area.

The joint government project, scheduled for completion by 1996, will affect one of the most scenic — if polluted — sections of the 1,770-mile Danube. The project is in a lush, 30-mile-wide section of wetland forest, a wildlife santuary penetrable only by canoe, between the Czechoslovakian city of Gabcikovo, near the Austrian border, and Nagymaros in Hungary. (66) ....B................ , because for decades it has been used as a dumping ground for urban, industrial and agricultural waste. But ecologists say that the project, which involves the construction of two hydro-electric power plants, two major dams and a shipping canal, will not only exacerbate that problem but in addition will severely blight the landscape.

When the project is in full operation, the dam at Gabcikovo will hold back the natural flow of water in order to create massive artificial floods that will sweep downriver morning and evening,

(67) ....A........ . Polluted sediment carried by the surging waters will be pushed up the Danube's tributaries. The twice-daily flooding will cause the tributary waters to flow the wrong way for several hours a day — (68) ....E.......... . But between the engineered floods, the Danube will be reduced to a trickle along the route, with most of the water stored in an artificial lake above the dam at Gabcikovo in preparation for another electricity-generating flood. Boats — mostly Soviet barges — navigating that portion of the river will be diverted through a canal on the Czechoslovakian side, barricaded by 60-foot-high asphalt walls lined with special plastic to resist chemical corrosion.

A which necessitates the building of dams up to 60 feet high to prevent unwanted flooding

B the river itself is already contaminated

C if you add up what the governments concerned have done between them

D when it is most urgently needed

E which in turn also means that the river's fish population will suffer dramatically

F but environmentalists in all three countries claim that

G despite serious scientific doubts to the contrary

H it has however been proved by scientists from both countries that

I if plans published recently are realised

J because of a controversial hydro-electric project launched by the governments of Hungary and Czechoslovakia

6 You and your flatmate are unhappy with the condition of the flat you are renting for a year. Your flatmate is especially angry and has listed the things wrong. Knowing that you are more diplomatic than he is, he has asked you to write to the landlord and request action. Write the letter.

Read his notes below.

You may add words and change the form of words where appropriate, but do not add any more ideas. Look carefully at the first note which has been expanded for you — number 69.

(69) *Heating system defective — can't tell if on or off.*

(70) *Water from kitchen taps — never more than trickle.*

(71) *Carpets — v. worn. Dangerous!*

(72) *Walls v. damp — health hazard?*

(73) *Draughts every room in house!*

(74) *Promised full sets cutlery and crockery — only a few items in fact.*

(75) *Front door hanging off! Easy for burglars.*

(76) *Pls. do something!*

You begin your letter like this: Dear Mr Ringfield,

I am writing to express our concern about the state of the above property which we have agreed to rent from you until 31 December this year.

(69) *The heating system seems to be defective and it is difficult at times to tell if it is on or off*

And you end it like this: Thank you for your attention in this matter.

Yours sincerely,

PAPER 4 : LISTENING

Time: Approx. 45 minutes

In this test you will hear four extracts of spoken English and you will be given time to choose your answers to the questions or to write answers. Before you listen to each extract, read the questions carefully. Read or look again while you are listening and choose **A, B, C** or **D,** complete the sentences, or do whatever you are asked to do. In **Section A, Section C** and **Section D** check your answers while you are listening for the second time. In **Section B** you will only hear the piece once.

Section A

Read the following information and questions 1–5. You're going to hear the last minute or two of an evening news bulletin on the radio. Listen to the recording and then answer questions 1–5. For each question decide which is the best answer, **A**, **B**, **C** or **D**. When you have finished, you'll hear the piece again.

1 Which two subjects are mentioned first?

A Football and politics.
B Nuclear power and scandals
C Television and hooligans.
D Defence policy and a British achievement.

2 How long had Grace been living in the same flat?

A 30 years.
B 81 years.
C 3 months.
D 75 years.

3 How did Grace die?

A She killed herself.
B She was killed.
C She died of shock.
D We don't know.

4 What was the coroner's reaction to her death?

A He thought it was criminal.
B He was amazed by the circumstances.
C He criticised the State for it.
D He thought it was understandable.

5 What was Grace's attitude to her neighbours?

A She was afraid of them.
B She didn't want any contact with them.
C She blamed them for her situation.
D She welcomed some of their efforts to help.

Section B

Read the form below and questions 6–13. Your name is Watkins and you work in the personal loans department of a bank. One customer, Mr France, has discussed a loan with you and some details have been filled in. Now you will hear a message from him on the office answerphone. Listen to the recording and, for questions 6–13 fill in the missing details on the form and change anything that needs to be changed in the light of what he says. Listen very carefully: you will hear this message only once.

Worldwide® Bank Inc.

Application for a Personal Loan

Full Name:	6	*Charles Enrico FRANCE*
Date of Birth:	7	30th June *18.03.46*
Address:		*Flat 3, 31, Broad Hill Road,*
		Bristol, Avon
Postcode:	8	BH8 3EY *BR6 6PU*
Telephone Number:		*Bristol 977324*
N.I. Number:	9	GJ 147680 VR
Passport Number:	10	WL 45098 E
Amount of loan:	11	17,000 8.12 year 79.50
Period of loan:	12	BH83EY
Purpose of loan:		*Purchase of caravan*
Monthly repayments:	13	~~15,000~~ 79.50
Signature(s) of applicant(s):		Anne IE Marie

Section C

Read the following information and questions 14–23. You're helping with a survey. As your colleague interviews a couple about their family car, its history and their plans for a new one, listen and fill in the form. Complete it according to what you hear. For questions 14–23 circle letters, tick boxes or write in as necessary. When you have finished, you'll hear the piece again.

14 How many cars does your household have?

☐ **a** 1 ☐ **b** 2 ☐ **c** 3+ ☐ **d** None

15 What make, model and type is the main car insured by your family?

a Make (e.g. Ford) ____________

b Model (e.g. Escort 1.3L) ____________

c Engine size (in cc's) ____________

16 Which registration letter is your car?

F ☐ ; **E** ☐ ; **D** ☐ ; **C** ☐ ; **B** ☐ ;

A ☐ ; **Y** ☐ ; **X** ☐ ; **W** ☐ ; Older ☐

17 Approximately when do you expect to replace the car?

☐☐ *Month* ☐☐ *Year*

18 What size is your next car likely to be?

Luxury (e.g. Jaguar, Mercedes) ☐

Executive (eg Rover 800, Granada, Carlton) ☐

Upper Medium (eg Cavalier, Sierra, Montego) ☐

Lower Medium (eg Escort, Rover 200, Astra) ☐

Small (eg Peugeot 205, Metro, Mini) ☐

19 Will the next car you buy be

☐ **a** New ☐ **b** Used

20 Will the car be

☐ **a** Yours ☐ **b** Company's

21 If company's, will you have the opportunity to choose the make and model of the car?

☐ **a** Yes ☐ **b** No

22 Who arranged your car insurance?

☐ **a** You ☐ **b** Partner

☐ **c** Empoyer ☐ **d** Other

23 Other than yourself, who is insured to drive your car?

☐ **a** Partner ☐ **b** Others (pls. state number) ☐ **c** Any

Section D

Questions 24–33. Read the following information and the lettered descriptions below. You're going to hear ten women talking about the subject of marriage. Listen, and for questions 24–33indicate the description of the speaker by putting the appropriate letter against the number of the speaker, for example Q against speaker 24, S against speaker 25, and so on. There are more descriptions than there are speakers on tape. When you have finished, you'll hear the piece again.

24 ...
25 ...
26 ...
27 ...
28 ...
29 ...
30 ...
31 ...
32 ...
33 ...

A This woman is a widow.

B This woman is keen to get married.

C This woman is married but not particularly happy

D This woman is divorced.

E This woman is probably engaged.

F This woman is a marriage guidance counsellor.

G This woman has not really thought about marriage yet.

H This woman could well be on her honeymoon.

I This woman will almost certainly never get married.

J This woman does not regret getting married.

K This woman is leading a campaign for 'battered wives'.

L This woman thinks she has a recipe for a good marriage.

M This woman hates men.

PAPER 5 : SPEAKING

Time: Approx. 15 minutes

Work in pairs throughout this Speaking Paper.

Phase A

Even though you might know each other well, do the following:

- Introduce yourself to your partner.
- Tell your partner something about yourself and what you do in your spare time.
- Ask your partner questions to find out more about how he or she likes to spend leisure time — both evenings and weekends.

Phase B

Student 1: turn to page 65. **Student 2:** turn to page 100.
Do not look at each other's material.

Phase C

Look at the advertisement opposite and discuss it as your teacher asks you to.

Phase D [Teacher]

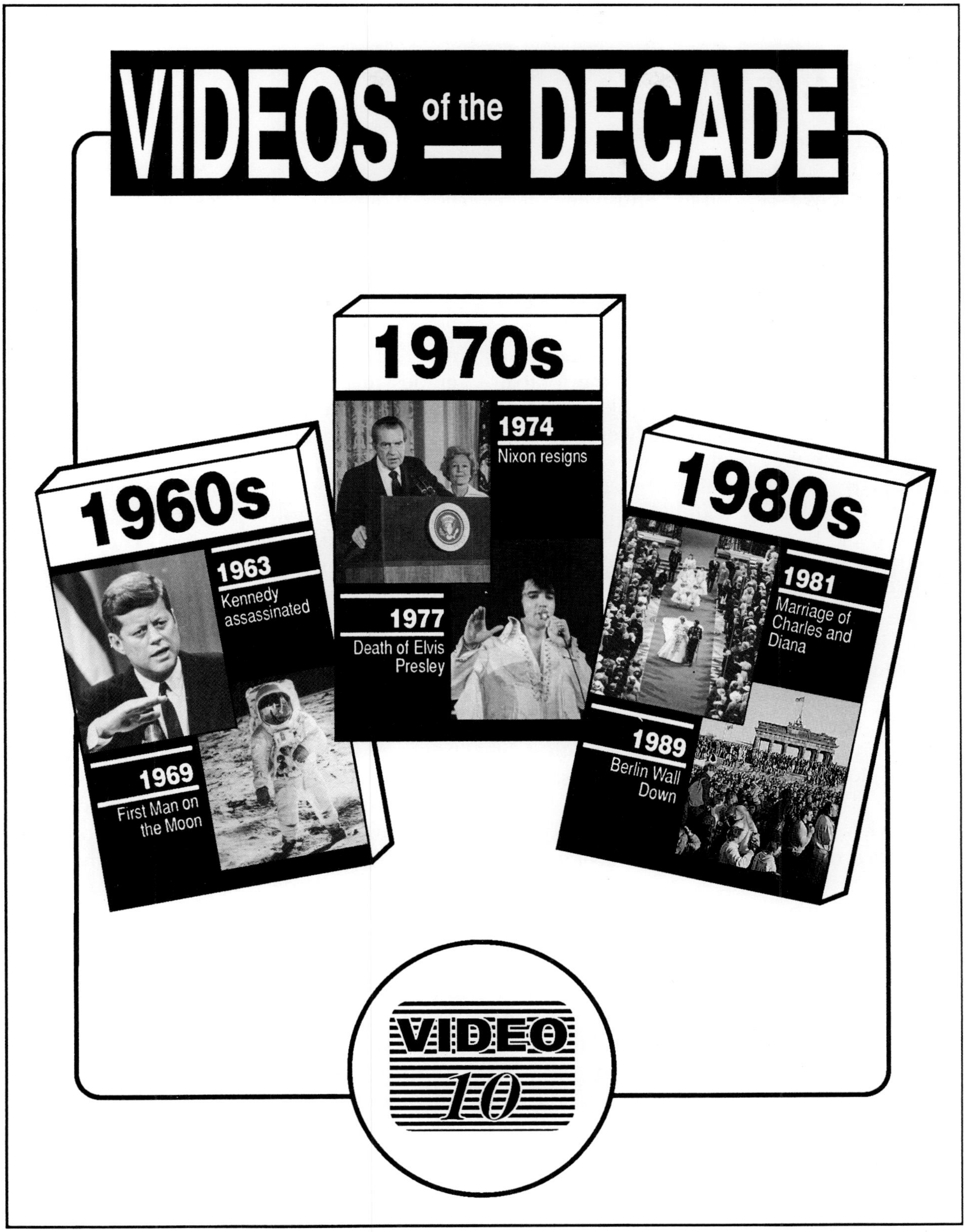
VIDEOS of the DECADE
1970s
1974
Nixon resigns
1977
Death of Elvis Presley
1960s
1963
Kennedy assassinated
1969
First Man on the Moon
1980s
1981
Marriage of Charles and Diana
1989
Berlin Wall Down
VIDEO
10

Exam Two

PAPER 1: READING

Time: 1 hour

1 Questions 1–6. Read this British newspaper article about American education Then choose the correct answers (**A**, **B**, **C** or **D**) for the questions that follow.

The All-American Way of Education

THE GOAL of most American teenagers is 'to be on the team'. Preferably the football team where they dress up like warriors from a space film and look twenty pounds heavier than they really are.

Sport rules school life. Classroom teachers cope daily with kids who are high. This could be caused by plain old narcotics, but the majority are high on sport. They race into class hot from Pep Assembly in a state of wild excitement and fidget through the lesson with pre-match nerves. Pep Assembly is an act of morning worship where the team members pledge allegiance to the flag, sing, dance, chant, wave arms, legs and anything else in celebration of their glorious team whom God is asked to bless. Underneath banners in childish scrawl, cheerleaders prance and pirouette and describe backflips whilst waving pom-poms and shouting 'Go, Pirates, go' or 'Charge, Cowboys, charge'.

In class teachers talk to themselves about civil wars and chemical compounds whilst pre-occupied students debate shotgun or blitz tactics or their chances of actually making it on to the field. Some know that even after all the rigorous training and the 30 minutes spent donning full padded kit, they may be one of the busload of anything up to 45 players who spend the whole match standing on the touchline.

School life is built around sport and academic work services it. A player cannot make the team unless s/he is attaining pass grades in all subjects. Proliferating stories about illiterate football players entering university or college on sports scholarships may be true; however, the pass-rate is usually just above the house-brick level.

This serves to show just how seriously the schools take their sport. The players and athletes endure a tough training schedule akin to the Marines, all done in their own time after lessons. Coaches are dedicated and demand and exact the standards expected of professional sports people. As a teacher in England who has listened to excuses about lame horses and boyfriends' 18th birthday parties when trying to muster a full rehearsal for a school play, I envy the sports coaches' authority. I also envy their fiscal reward. Although I suspect they would do it for nothing, the teacher turned coach receives extra pay for running a team. There are rewards for able and dedicated team members too — the pride of being in the team, the right to wear the prized special jacket if one achieves varsity status, and, ultimately, a college or university scholarship. With tuition fees running at $20,000 a year for top universities, it's no wonder that parents encourage their offspring to kick a ball instead of writing a poem.

At my first match at my husband's small high school (only 450 pupils) I had been amazed to see the public buying entrance tickets, surprised to hear the school band in full uniform playing in the stands, fascinated to watch the acrobatic antics of cheerleaders, interested to see an electronic scoreboard, the hot dog and popcorn stands and the press box. I was absolutely stunned eight games later to hear that the football season had ended. All that exclusively designed padded kit and protective headgear and razzamatazz for nine games and four of those away. The schools can justify the expense because it builds team and school spirit and because they raise much of the money themselves. School football is high profile. A local video store provides sponsorship, and plastic cups printed with the team's logo and the store's particulars are used for match beverages.

Much to my amazement the school did not fall apart at the end of the football season when basketball and wrestling took over. Many teachers despair that sport seems to take precedence over their lessons. They struggle to teach pupils who divide their energies between the team and their night job in the local supermarket.

The teachers agree, however, that sport does build team spirit and gives the students comradeship and a sense of belonging and pride in their school. It is, in fact, heartwarming to see the strong friendships and enthusiasms that develop on and off the field in American high schools and it does make me think about the cold-toed mornings I spent as a solitary parent on the touchline of a school football match in England, cheering on my son and totally embarrassing him. A bit more pride and enthusiasm might not go amiss on our school playing fields or in our assemblies.

1 'Pep Assembly' would appear to be

A a rather wild concert.
B a private team talk on game tactics.
C a practice and training session.
D a ritual for team members and supporters.

2 What are typical lessons like?

A Teachers teach but pupils' minds are elsewhere.
B Teachers and pupils discuss sport.
C Pupils are bored, particularly in chemistry and history.
D Pupils reluctantly do what they are told.

3 What is the connection between sport and US colleges and universities?

A The best players wear a special jacket there.
B A lot of illiterate students are there just to play sport.
C Many good players go on to study sport there.
D Top sports players receive money to study there.

4 The writer was absolutely amazed at

A how much equipment was needed for the team.
B how short the football season was.
C how many other sports were played.
D how much money the school made from the games.

5 Which of these factors makes teaching difficult in the US?

A A lot of pupils cannot read or write very well.
B Parents do not encourage their children to study .
C Children spend too much time watching television.
D Many pupils are tired from working to earn money.

6 The writer's overall impression is that American schools

A have something English schools could benefit from.
B achieve a sensible balance between sport and academic work.
C have high standards of teaching.
D emphasise the difference between winners and losers.

2 Read this article from the first 1990 issue of the American magazine *Newsweek* and then answer the questions that follow it.

ROBOTS

have been the stuff of popular culture for so long that we think of them mostly as fun. In the next decade they will finally become practicable beyond factory assembly lines. Granted, they won't perform the wondrous stunts they do in sci-fi movies; the first generation of 'real' robots may seem a bit crude. But by the end of the decade we may well encounter tiny robots cooking hamburgers in fast-food restaurants, mopping up shopping malls, even delivering meal trays in hospitals.

Two factors are pushing the development of robotics technology and economics. Artificial intelligence is the key to a successful robot, but some of the simplest tasks for a human mind are difficult for a robot. One example: the ability to look at the corner of a room, where walls and ceiling meet, and know that the corner goes in, not out. Easy for humans, very tough for real-world R2D2s. But new computers, which more closely resemble the human brain, look particularly promising for teaching the robots how to adapt to their surroundings. Someday robots may have enough (artificial) sense to, say, vacuum the carpet in a simple office without knocking over the water cooler, at least not more than once.

Economics is the key to the acceptance of robots. As declining birthrates lead to a shortage of entry-level workers in much of the industrialised world, researchers are designing robots that can manage at least portions of such jobs as burger flippers or hospital orderlies. The robot orderly, for example, can deliver meals and prescriptions; it still can't make the bed. Fast-food robots will probably cook and package food; humans will still greet the public at the counter and give incorrect change.

By the late '90s, improved robots will be inexpensive enough to serve as aides for the disabled, giving even quadruplegics the ability to feed themselves and perform office work. Not all robots will be so benign. Another model in production is a security guard designed to wander deserted warehouses and signal a human guard when it encounters intruders. At least one American firm has designed an armed security robot capable of firing a weapon.

And the long-promised human robot? This little electronic servant, capable of delivering a frosty beer from the fridge, picking up the kids' toys and washing the occasional window, probably won't be a mass-market item in the '90s — unless we modify our homes to accommodate them. Every room would need to have tiny radio beacons to tell the robot where it is and staircases would need special construction for easy robot access. Sound unlikely? Perhaps. But in 1890 a person might have thought it unlikely if he had been told that the entire urban landscape of the planet would be modified to accommodate the automobile.

R2D2: One of the (now famous) robot characters in the film *Star Wars*

Questions 7–11. From the list a–l on the right (below) choose the most appropriate heading to summarise each of the five paragraphs of the article.

7 .... Paragraph **1**

8 .... Paragraph **2**

9 .... Paragraph **3**

10... Paragraph **4**

11... Paragraph **5**

a Robots for the home
b Dangerous robots
c Robots in films
d The importance of artificial intelligence
e New developments in robot technology
f The cheapness of the new robot
g Cars and robots
h Robots become a feature of everyday life
i Jobs that robots will and will not be able to take over
j Robots instead of people
k Humans are more efficient in burger bars and hospitals
l Friendly and unfriendly robots

Questions 12–17. According to the article, which of the following list of jobs (a–j) will robots probably be doing in the 1990s? (6 answers)

12....

13....

14....

15....

16....

17....

a giving change in cafés
b handing out medicines in hospitals
c vacuuming offices
d working on factory assembly lines
e fetching drinks from the fridge
f making beds in hospitals
g helping handicapped people
h cleaning pavements
i preparing food in cafés
j acting as security guards

Questions 18–20. Which of the following list (a–g) does the article mention as causing problems in the development of robots? (3 answers)

18....

19....

20....

a Robots can't give the correct change
b Robots cannot perceive the world as humans can
c Robots can't climb ordinary stairs
d Robots can't talk
e Robots can only do simple jobs
f Robots could not operate in the ordinary homes of today
g Robots are very expensive

3 **Read this short story from a popular magazine. The story is set at Christmas, a time when children are traditionally brought presents by a mythical figure called Father Christmas or Santa Claus. Father Christmas dresses in red and has a long white beard; he comes from the Arctic Circle and drives a reindeer sledge carrying all his presents across the sky.**

What a day for a bailiff ...

by Martin Plimmer

Keep your head down for long enough and Christmas will eventually go away. That was my family's attitude. Some old films on television, a quiz show, some comedy programmes and it's all over. The real world intruded occasionally into this reverie; the twins would swallow holly, grandfather would fall asleep in the snow, Aunt Mona would leave the plastic giblets bag in the turkey. But with single-mindedness you could devote most of your attention to the box, saving your strength for the channel wars when half the family wanted BBC1 and half wanted Channel 4.

That was an ordinary Christmas. Last Christmas at Uncle Clarence's something extraordinary happened. None of us will ever be the same again.

There was a ring on the bell in mid-Christmas Eve viewing. You know how your heart jumps when you're not expecting visitors, especially at Christmas when normal people are at home watching television. It's got to be something pretty horrible out there — a masked gunman, perhaps.

It was a bailiff. Unpaid credit card, he said. He took the television away.

We were relatively snug until then. We were happily watching an old film. All was calm, all was quiet. Well, the twins were doing something noisy with a pair of nutcrackers and a cat but that was normal. We were all ignoring everybody else, even the twins, who we could tell apart this year as one was sprayed silver.

That apart, Uncle Clarence's house was not festive nor joyful. You could tell life had passed Uncle Clarence by. It was as if he had a badge saying 'Life has passed me by'. He compensated himself by buying electronic gadgets which gave him unjoyful satisfaction. This year he had bought an electronic fairy for his Christmas tree. Every hour it would kick its legs up into the air for 30 seconds before settling down again to all our relief. What made Uncle Clarence beautiful in our eyes was his satellite TV. You could flip from a comedy programme in Dutch to an American news report about the latest mass murder. He was very proud of this facility and we were keen to share it. The whole family had turned up, even poor Joy (despite her hernia).

The bailiff was unreasonably cheerful when he burst in, fresh as frost, that night. Bailiffs are like that nowadays as though they're bringing you something nice instead of taking it away. They learn that at bailiff school. Sometimes you can even hear them whistling up the path, like milkmen from hell. 'I'll have the TV' he said, then boomed 'Merry Christmas' and bustled out.

We had all stood up. The remote control sat alone on the couch. Uncle Clarence wrapped it in tissue and placed it tenderly in a big china jar. I'll never forget the sound of Uncle Clarence sobbing. But what followed was worse. Complete silence.

The consequence was awful. Two days of each other's conversation. This had never happened in living memory. Few could remember the last time my father had uttered more than ten words in a row. There wasn't a sound in Uncle Clarence's house for 20 long painful minutes. You could have heard a pine needle drop. We all flinched suddenly when the electronic fairy which Uncle Clarence had placed at the top of his tree suddenly whirred into its dancing routine and then shuddered right off its perch and onto the floor.

Then something extraordinary happened. A gurgling sound no one had ever heard before welled out of poor Joy. She was laughing. Then we were all laughing. Then, out of the blue, Aunt Mona told a funny story. She wasn't frowning any more. We laughed more. The house was full of babble. Kate sang a Christmas song. Then Uncle Clarence got up and produced a ping-pong ball from behind his ear. No-one knew he had it in him.

Later my father told stories about the war. My father never talks about the war. At midnight, filled with a sense of wonder, we toasted Christmas Day. Then we roared off to bed.

That was a Christmas all right. My relatives shake their heads now when they talk of it. It gave us all strength. I think about it more than anyone. I was the one who followed the bailiff out that night to shut the gate. I was sure he hadn't noticed me. I watched him go down the street and heave Uncle Clarence's television into the back of a red removal lorry. Then I watched him take off his bailiff jacket and stuff it in a dustbin.

He was wearing red underneath. I hadn't noticed the beard before. He fiddled for keys and unlocked the cab. His breath was frost white. He climbed in, turned his head to where I stood behind the hedge and winked. As he pulled away I noticed the Lapland number plates. He then took off into the air and quickly disappeared over the church tower.

bailiff: In Britain, an official who can come to your house to remove possessions if you fail to pay your debts.

Questions 21–25. Look at statements a–k on the right. Which five are true about most Christmases?

Questions 26–30. Look at statements a–k on the right. Which five are true about the Christmas in the story?

21 ...	**a**	The family had a very happy time.
22 ...	**b**	The family had a lot of visitors.
23 ...	**c**	They watched television most of the time.
24 ...	**d**	They talked to each other a great deal.
25 ...	**e**	They had a delicious meal.
	f	They argued about what to look at on TV.
26 ...	**g**	There were a series of minor disasters.
27 ...	**h**	Father Christmas took the TV away.
28 ...	**i**	They didn't enjoy themselves very much.
29 ...	**j**	Several different generations of the family got together.
30 ...	**k**	The author's father had a lot to say.

Questions 31–42. Now look at the list of statements below (a–l) about people from the story. Match the people on the left with the statements about them. Note that in some cases there are two or three answers for each person — so your answers will be 31-42.

Uncle Clarence (3 answers)	31 ...	**a**	... was really Father Christmas.
	32 ...	**b**	... told a joke.
	33 ...	**c**	... reminisced about the past.
The twins (2 answers)	34 ...	**d**	... saw the bailiff drive away.
	35 ...	**e**	... never usually laughed.
The author of the story	36 ...	**f**	... tormented the cat.
The bailiff	37 ...	**g**	... was not in good health.
The author's father	38 ...	**h**	... had a very special television.
Joy (2 answers)	39 ...	**i**	... was not a very careful cook.
	40 ...	**j**	... did some magic tricks.
Aunt Mona (2 answers)	41 ...	**k**	... often got into trouble.
	42 ...	**l**	... burst into tears.

4 Questions 43–57. Find the answers to the following questions in the article from *Green Magazine* on these pages. Write the letter of each paragraph in the space beside each question.

Which paragraph

— describes safe computer cleaners?	43 ...
— gives the ecological angle on photocopying?	44 ...
— suggests an alternative method of cleaning phone handsets?	45 ...
— praises a firm for respecting birds?	46 ...
— suggests a way of absorbing the chemical, formaldehyde?	47 ...
— quotes a company being frank about its anti-environmental stand?	48 ...
— refers to the fact that not all paper can be recycled? (3 answers)	49 ...
	50 ...
	51 ...
— suggests where you can find out whether paper can be recycled or not?	52 ...
— explains why solvents are environmentally harmful?	53 ...
— refers to manufacturers who behave in a rather uneconomical way?	54 ...
— refers specifically to a particular kind of tree? (2 answers)	55 ...
	56 ...
— both praises and criticises one particular product?	57 ...

BASKET CASES

How officious is your office? While you're filling in those forms, you might be filling up with form-aldehyde.

Clara Bayley finds that work CAN be bad for you.

A Lots of office products contain solvents which give off ozone when exposed to light. The ozone, unfortunately, can't float up towards the ozone layer and help to fill the gap - at lower levels it collects to form photochemical smog which is damaging to human and plant life.

B Everyone likes to have plants around the office, but the spider plant serves an extraordinary purpose quite apart from looking pretty. It will absorb formaldehyde, one of the most prevalent indoor pollutants often found in particle-board furniture.

Columbia International has produced solvent-free liquid paper, Opti. The company has also produced several ranges of cleansing equipment for computers which do not contain toxic substances and use non-CFC pump action propellants. **C**

Many cleaning products use CFCs (the guilty chemicals for ozone destruction) as propellants in the aerosols. We all know that telephone receivers can get quite unpleasant, but why not try warm, soapy water instead of germicidal spray? **D**

Two hundred and fifty trees are felled every five minutes to satisfy our paper demands, but many products from **Universal** are made of recycled paper. Alternative methods to chlorine bleaching are being pioneered to avoid the production of dioxins. Wasted paper in offices reaches horrifying levels, but not all paper is suitable for recycling. FoE produce a useful guide. **E**

Sellotape is made from biodegradable cellulose, which comes from eucalyptus woodpulp - the trees are pruned, but not felled, although eucalypts can be an environmental problem in some countries. Cellulose biodegrades down into water and carbon dioxide within six months. The glue is put onto the tape with the virtuous hot-metal method, which doesn't use solvents. No prizes for overpackaging, however. **F**

The good old fashioned alternatives to throw-away pens are still available. **Staedtler** makes its pencils of cedar wood from California, where the trees grow fast. They replant as they chop down, and even claim to have left uncropped an area of 25,000 acres in their cedar forest because the endangered lesser spotted long-eared owl was found to be nesting there. **G**

A well known company unsurprisingly had "No Comment" to make about the wastefulness and environmentally hostile nature of their disposable plastic pens. There was a similar response from a typewriter ribbon manufacturer, which candidly admitted it was "not in their interest" to make them re-inkable. The more ribbons you throw away, the more profit they rake in. **H**

Environment-friendly sticky labels are a big problem. The waxy backing-paper is very hard to recycle, as are fax paper, tracing paper and other kinds with a shiny surface. And, although it is actually cheaper to use a hot-metal process to apply the glue to the label, most manufacturers still use solvents in the process. **I**

Photocopiers and laser printers are a menace not just because the toners they use are harmful solvents. They also demand very thick, very white paper which is hard to produce without using chlorine bleaches and virgin pulp. One manufacturer explained, "with equipment worth thousands of pounds, a customer would rather chop down a few trees than risk it breaking down by using a recycled paper". **J**

PAPER 2: WRITING

Time: 2 hours

Section A

You are staying in London for a time. This is part of a letter you receive from a friend who is soon coming to visit you while you are there. Your friend wants to work in the Wardrobe Department of the National Theatre in your country when he/she leaves college.

I'll be in London from late Tuesday evening till Friday morning and would love to go to some plays. I can't stand musicals or comedies. What I really like is serious drama. What do you recommend? And do you think it might be possible to do a tour of the National Theatre some time?

Opposite are some extracts from the theatre review section of a magazine showing you what is on at the moment. **You do not need to read the extracts in detail.**

You telephone another friend, John, who is very keen on the theatre and who you know will have seen many of the plays advertised and may be able to give you some advice. Here are some notes that you make after your telephone call.

'Temptation' — has had some bad reviews but J. thinks it's great.
Must see 'Racing Demon' if at all poss.
J. also v. enthusiastic about 'Les Miserables' — it's by far the best musical he's ever seen.
'Shadowlands' — rather depressing but v. interesting.
'Cats' — another must if you like musicals.
'The Wild Duck' — highly recommended.
'Run for Your Wife' — very funny.
'The Mousetrap' — a classic detective story. J. liked it very much when he saw it 30 years ago but he was only 10 at the time!

Read all the information on these pages carefully and then write:

1 a letter to your friend suggesting what plays you would recommend seeing when and why.

2 a letter to the National Theatre asking whether they will be doing any tours at the time when your friend is going to be in London and explaining the kind of thing that he or she is particularly interested in.

National Theatre, Cottesloe

South Bank, SE1 (071 928 2252) Waterloo tube. National Theatre Company. See also Lyttelton, Olivier.
Weds (27), Wed (4): **'Racing Demon'** by David Hare, directed by Richard Eyre with Michael Bryant, David Bamber, Oliver Ford Davies. A gripping exploration of the maelstrom of evangelical conviction politics that's tearing the liberal heart out of the Church of England, symbolised by the ageing humanist Rev Lionel Espy's gradual usurpation from his inner-city parish by his young charismatic counter-part, Rev Tony Ferris. Couched in exquisite humour and acute arguments, Hare could not have asked for a better cast or director to tease out the nuance, subtlety and passionate humanism of his script. 7.30pm, Wed (27) Mat 2.30pm. £8.50; student standby £5; restricted views £6.50.

Palace

Shaftesbury Avenue, W1 (071 434 0909) Leicester Square tube.
'Les Miserables' RSC transfer of British première of the musical by Alain Boublil and Claude-Michel Schonberg, lyrics by Herbert Kretzmer based on the novel by Victor Hugo. Directed by Trevor Nunn and John Caird. With Oystein Wiik, David Burt and Linzi Hateley. This highly theatrical production has stormed barricades all over the world. Mon-Sat 7.30pm. Thur, Sat Mat 2.30pm. £5.50-£25. (Booking to April '91)

Phoenix Theatre

Charing Cross Road, WC2 (071 867 1044) Leicester Square tube.
'The Wild Duck' by Ibsen, presented by the Peter Hall Company and Triumph Theatre Productions, directed by Peter Hall, designed by John Bury, with Alex Jennings and David Threlfall. A rare outing for Ibsen's most Chekhovian tragi-comedy where the uncompromising Gregers forces the Ekdal family to realise that their happiness is built upon a shaky foundation of lies and deceit. A rigorous, illuminating experience in which Threlfall and Jennings excell, and a production that refuses to romanticise any of the characters and seems entirely in harmony with Ibsen's extraordinary ability to make you laugh and cry simultaneously. Mon-Sat 7.30pm; Thur & Sat Mat 2.30pm. £8-£16. (Booking to August 4)

St Martin's

West Street, Cambridge Circus, WC2 (071 836 1443) Leicester Square tube.
'The Mousetrap' by Agatha Christie, directed by Kim Grant. 35 years old, the world's longest running play and still no end in sight. Mon-Sat 8pm; Tue Mat 2.45pm, Sat Mat 5pm. £6-£14.50. (Runs 2¼hrs)

Queen's

Shaftesbury Avenue, W1 (071 734 1166/071 439 3849) Leicester Square tube.
'Shadowlands' by William Nicholson, directed by Elijah Moshinsky, designed by Mark Thompson. Story of CS Lewis's relationship with the American poet Joy Davidman and how her eventual death by cancer led him to reconsider many of his previously held beliefs. A model of directorial discretion, packed with emotional bombshells, painful social clashes, harrowing hospital trips and two marvellous performances by Nigel Hawthorne and Jane Lapotaire. Mon-Sat 8pm; Wed Mat 3pm; Sat Mat 4.30pm. £7-£16.50. (Booking to July 28)

New London

Drury Lane, WC2 (071 405 0072) Covent Garden tube.
'Cats' by Andrew Lloyd Webber. Directed by Trevor Nunn. Choreography by Gillian Lynne. The dancing moggie show. Continuing run of this hugely successful adaptation of TS Eliot's cat poems which has cruised past the record for London's longest-ever running musical held previously by 'Jesus Christ, Superstar'. It's now been on its feet for nine years. Mon-Sat 7.45pm; Sat Mat 3pm. £7-£20. (Runs 2¾hrs/Booking to Jan 26 '91)

Westminster Theatre

Palace Street, SW1 (071 834 0283/cc 071 834 0048). Victoria tube/BR.
'Temptation' by Václav Havel, translated by George Theiner, directed by James Roose-Evans, designed by Bruno Santini and Mike Roberts, music by Kevin Malpass. Disappointments abound in Roose-Evans's flamboyant and studiously wacky production which glosses dark political undercurrents with grotesque comic veneers which fail to capture the Kafka-esque fears and cowardly deceits of a world structured on dictatorial power. Mon-Sat 7.45pm; Wed & Sat Mats 3pm. Mon-Thur £8-£14.50; Fri, Sat £8-£15.50. (Runs 2hrs 15mins/Booking to August)

Aldwych

The Aldwych, WC2 (071 836 6404) Covent Garden tube.
'Run For Your Wife' by Ray Cooney. Commercial farce about a man with two wives; bad jokes, clever comedy. With Eric Sykes, Terry Scott, Derek Griffiths, Jacqueline Clarke, Judy Graham and Ron Aldridge. Mon-Fri 8pm; Thur Mat 2.30pm; Sat 5.30pm & 8.30pm. £7.50-£15. (Runs 2¼hrs/Booking to Sept 15)

Section B

Choose **ONE** of the following writing tasks. Your answer should follow exactly the instructions given. You are advised to write approximately 250 words.

1

The Chance of a Lifetime
Win the holiday house of your dreams! Write a 250-word description of what your ideal house would be like, where it would be and how you would use it. We will make the dream come true for the person who, in the opinion of our judges, writes the best description.

You decide to enter this competition. **Write your entry.**

2 This is part of a letter that you receive from a friend. **Read it and write a reply.**

I really don't know what to do. Both sets of parents are against our getting married — they say we should wait until we've both finished college and got good jobs. I suspect they think we may change our minds but I'm sure we shan't. I know that neither of us will ever want to marry anyone else. It would be difficult getting married now — we'd probably have to live with my parents for the next couple of years — but surely it'd be better than not being together while we're young? What do you think? I'd really welcome your advice as you always seem to see things so clearly.

3 You have been asked to write an article for a general interest English-language magazine about the system of education in your country. It has been suggested that you should write a brief summary of the structure of the education system and then concentrate on what you see as being the strong points and the problems of education in your country at the moment. **Write your article.**

4 You are interested in finding a job abroad for three months. You see this advertisement in a newspaper.

Would you like to find a job abroad?

We specialise in matching people to jobs throughout the world.

We can help you find either temporary or permanent posts and through us you can gain access to many kinds of jobs in many different countries.

If you are interested, write to us, giving full details of your qualifications, interests and experience, tell us what kind(s) of work you might be interested in, why you want to work abroad and where you would like to work. The more information you can give us, the easier it will be for us to find the best work for you.

Write a letter to the agency.

PAPER 3: ENGLISH IN USE

Time: 1 hour 30 minutes

Section A

1 Complete the following article by writing the missing words in the spaces provided. Use **only one word** in each space. The first one has been done for you as an example.

Still-life Study with Bleeps

Psychologists in Sheffield are discovering how young people spend their lives by bleeping them at random hours of the day or night. When the pager sounds, volunteers must whip out their diaries and write down *what* (1) they are doing, no .... (2) what they are doing. The psychologists insist that, ... (3) embarassing it may be, the subjects are expected to answer the questions: What were you doing? What were you feeling .... (4)? What were you thinking about? And did you feel happy, sad, tense or relaxed?

His volunteers, of both sexes and .... (5) between 17 and 20, include people .... (6) full-time employment, work trainees and the unemployed. They have to wear the pager and carry the diary for a week .... (7) which they are bleeped eight times .... (8) random every day.

'This method .... (9) study is unique in Britain', Dr Evans of Sheffield University .... (10) the annual meeting of the British Psychological Society in Cumbria yesterday. 'It enables us to interpret on-going behaviour.'

The results of the one-year project .... (11) intended to combat stress .... (12) the fact that people are deeply stressed by .... (13) their lives interrupted by a bleep. Dr Evans described the pagers as the ideal tool for .... (14) a picture of young people's lives over a typical week.

However, catching his subjects unawares has not produced any shocking revelations. 'One of our .... (15) so far is that young people's lifestyles are not radically different from .... (16) they were ten years ago', said Dr Evans.

2 Read the article below and, in the items opposite, circle the letter next to the word which best fits each space. The first one has been done for you as an example.

A Freezer Full of Books

A SWEDISH MONASTERY has demonstrated to scientists the advantage of freezing books in order to preserve them. The monastery .... (17) at Skoklosters Slott is .... (18) in an unheated room with open grilles. In winter the temperature inside falls below -10° Centigrade which is extremely uncomfortable for the .... (19) but ideal for the books, which have .... (20) remarkably well over 300 years.

Storage at low temperatures slows down the .... (21) at which acid attacks paper and brings down relative humidity, reducing .... (22) to both ink and binding. Photographs and microfilm, which are even less durable, also .... (23) longer in cold storage.

'Freezing in cold storage certainly helps preserve material, but the difficulties .... (24) when you want to use it', says Marie Jackson of the National Preservation Office. Libraries abroad have already begun to build cold storage .... (25). The greatest investment has been made by the National Library of Australia in Canberra, which recently built over three kilometres of shelf .... (26) for storing only low-use material at 8° Centigrade. Material required by readers first has to be .... (27) for 24 hours at 16° Centigrade.

Most of the original material in the cold store has already been microfilmed and the originals are .... (28) rarely required. Master copies of microfilm are also .... (29) in the cold store with a working film kept at .... (30) temperature.

The National Preservation Office is following Canberra's work with interest. 'They are at the .... (31) of preservation techniques, but so far no libraries in Britain have .... (32) for cold storage', Ms Jackson said.

17	**A** bookshop	**B** study	**C** library	**D** office
18	**A** roomed	**B** placed	**C** positioned	**D** housed
19	**A** monkeys	**B** monks	**C** monarchs	**D** monsters
20	**A** lived	**B** preserved	**C** survived	**D** persisted
21	**A** rate	**B** extent	**C** degree	**D** amount
22	**A** wounds	**B** damage	**C** injuries	**D** hurt
23	**A** take	**B** last	**C** remain	**D** go
24	**A** go	**B** happen	**C** realise	**D** come
25	**A** amenities	**B** equipment	**C** facilities	**D** provisions
26	**A** cases	**B** space	**C** place	**D** length
27	**A** accustomed	**B** cooked	**C** melted	**D** acclimatised
28	**A** therefore	**B** however	**C** moreover	**D** nevertheless
29	**A** taken	**B** held	**C** had	**D** arrested
30	**A** house	**B** room	**C** library	**D** inside
31	**A** forehead	**B** foreground	**C** forefront	**D** forehand
32	**A** opted	**B** chosen	**C** selected	**D** decided

Section B

3 In most lines of the following text there is one mistake with a verb. It is either the wrong tense or is in some other way in the wrong form for its context.

Read the text, put a line through each incorrect verb and then write the correct form of the verb in the space provided at the end of the line. Some lines are correct. Indicate these lines with a tick (√) in the space provided. The first line has been done as an example.

I hated skiing the first time I tried it. Now I ~~am wondering~~ how (33) *wonder*

I could ever *not* have enjoyed it. True, you usually end the (34) ....

day feel wet and stiff. But the exhilaration of standing on a (35) √

mountain slope breathing clear air make it worth every aching (36) breath

muscle. Skiing feels as close as you can get to flying under (37) could

your own steam. Not immediately, of course. Everyone fall (38) falls

frequently at first, and I had been no exception. The second year (39) have been

I went skiing I have even broken my leg. But I was already in (40) broken

love with the sport by then and it certainly didn't stop me (41) √

to take the fastest train to the ski slopes at the next opportunity. (42) √

Why I like it so much? I think it's partly because in the (43) do I like

mountains there is places where you can't hear a car even in the (44) are

distance. And the snow is so clean and different from the grey (45) √

slush we are used to have in cities. Now I would very much (46) are

rather to be on top of a snowy mountain than in any city street. (47) √

As soon as winter begins I feel it's time I head for the mountains (48) √

again.

4 You are reading a newspaper when a friend asks you what news there is. You put some of the headlines into normal English for him or her. This means adding extra words and putting verbs into an appropriate form. In some cases you will also have to change words in the headlines from typical newspaper words to ordinary English words. The words which need changing have been underlined. **You will not need to add more than two words in any gap.** The first has been done for you as an example.

THREE <u>PERISH</u> IN ROME HOTEL BLAZE

Three (49 *people died* ___ in a fire in a hotel in Rome yesterday.

EXPERTS CLAIM WORLD HEADING FOR OIL PRICES <u>SLUMP</u>

Experts claim that the world is heading for a (50) ______________ the price of oil.

PM ANNOUNCES £9 MILLION <u>SCHEME</u> TO HELP ELDERLY

The Prime Minister yesterday announced a (51) ________________spend £9 million to help (52) ________________ .

SMITH: NO POINT IN DRUGS

Yesterday John Smith said that (53) ____________ no point (54) ____________ drugs.

China <u>Vows</u> To Back UN Peace <u>Moves</u>

Last night China (55) ______________ support proposals for peace (56) ____________ by the United Nations.

Section C

5 Choose the best phrase or sentence (from **A–J** given below) to fit each of the numbered blanks in the following passage. (The passage is the beginning of an article in a business review magazine.) Four of the suggested answers do not fit at all. Write the letter of the missing phrase in the appropriate blank.

PLANNING AHEAD

THE KEY TO HIRING A TEMPORARY EMPLOYEE

Getting maximum results from a professional temporary worker — or 'temp' for short — depends a great deal on advance planning.

Many office situations require temporary help. A changeover from a manual to a computerised file system, for example, requires trained data entry operators to move the bulk of information (57) .... Combining two branch offices requires the consolidation of many records. Any big change in operating procedures or equipment calls for extra help, (58) .... If specifics are well thought out ahead of time, main problem areas can be avoided from the beginning.

1 *Have the project clearly in mind.* A temp's workday begins when she or he checks in, (59) .... while department heads decide what is to be done. Plan ahead at least a day before, and consider whether more than one department will be affected.

If a supervisor or secretary is responsible for the temp, make it clear that, as a manager, you are delegating the authority. (60) .... so there won't be needless breaks in the workflow for questions that should have been addressed earlier.

2 *Have a work space prepared.* It is best to have the temp sit at the same desk for the duration of the assignment. This eliminates a lost half-hour each morning in an office-wide discussion (61) .... , as well as moving all the supplies to a new place. Full preparation includes supplies. Many temps carry their own small items, but it is better if you provide such items as pens, pencils and erasers.

3 *Co-ordinate.* If a temp has to use certain equipment, consult the schedules of the employees who would normally use this equipment (62) ....

(63) .... one employee in the morning and another in the afternoon, a three-hour task shouldn't be assigned half an hour before lunch. Tug-of-war between too many bosses wastes everybody's time.

- **A** to ensure the temp fits smoothly into the office workflow
- **B** the employee should fully understand the project
- **C** by using a quick checklist like this
- **D** about where the temporary employee will sit
- **E** while waiting to decide what must be done
- **F** so that regular help is free to process current work
- **G** whereas the agency that sent her/him should check this
- **H** if the temp is to help
- **I** as does seasonal work during vacation and holidays
- **J** yet many report they are kept idle for the first hour

6 You answered the telephone on behalf of a friend of yours and made some quick notes during the call. Now you have to transform the notes into sentences in order to leave a clear message for your friend. Change each of the notes into a complete sentence. The first one has been done for you as an example.

Sergio Rossi.

(64) *Looking forward meeting you Monday.*

(65) *Arrive airport 11.15, flight SA 211.*

(66) *Recognise him — 1m.60cms., blond, round glasses, black briefcase, two grey and red suitcases.*

(67) *S's secretary booked room Walton Hotel.*

(68) *Please check — shower, telephone, t.v. in room, vegetarian meals available.*

(69) *Yesterday Board of Directors agree plans?*

(70) *S's wife home all day — please ring with answers to above qs.*

(71) *Sergio bring anything your wife or children?*

(72) *Apols. trouble you — so many questions.*

Dear Kurt,

Sergio Rossi rang while I was here and asked me to give you quite a detailed message.

(64) *He's looking forward to seeing you on Monday*

(65) ____________________

(66) ____________________

(67) ____________________

(68) ____________________

(69) ____________________

(70) ____________________

(71) ____________________

(72) ____________________

I hope all this is clear. If not, call me when you get back.

PAPER 4 : LISTENING

Time: Approx. 45 minutes

In this test you will hear four extracts of spoken English and you will be given time to choose your answers to the questions or to write answers. Before you listen to each extract, read the questions carefully. Read or look again while you are listening and choose **A, B, C** or **D**, complete the sentences, or do whatever you are asked to do. In **Section A, Section C** and **Section D** check your answers while you are listening for the second time. In **Section B** you will only hear the piece once.

Section A

Read the following information and questions 1-13. You're going to hear part of a lecture about great film actors of the century. This part is about Charles Laughton. Listen, and for questions 1-13 complete the notes with information you hear about him. Don't worry about the spelling of names and so on. When you have finished, you'll hear the piece again.

Dates 1 1899.

Country of birth 2 England

Nationality 3 ~~England~~ America

First acting work 4 ______

Wife's name 5 ______

Date of marriage 6 1929.

Name and date of first Hollywood film 7 The old dark house 8 1933.

Is particularly noted for his performances as 9 ______

Date of founding own film company 10 1955 1938

Name of own film company 11 British

Name of film he directed 12 Make flowers

Name of his last film 13 Adviser and concides.

Section B

Read the following information and look at pictures 14–21. You're going to listen to a man who has had the embarassing experience of leaving his car keys inside his locked car. He gives advice on both how to deal with and how to avoid this situation. Some of the pictures match what the speaker says and others don't. Listen, and for questions 14–21 tick (√) just those pictures which match the advice he gives. Listen very carefully: you will hear this talk only once.

14 ☐

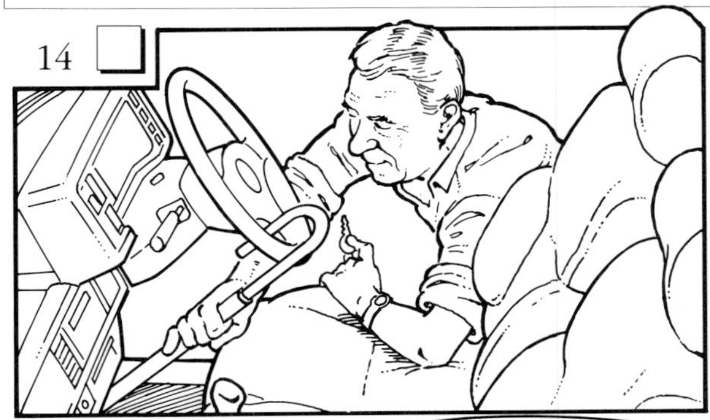

15 ☐

16 ☐

17 ☐

18 ☐

19 ☐

20 ☐

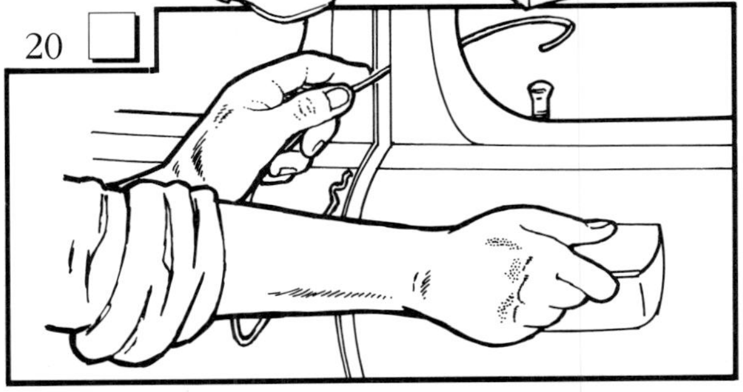

21 ☐

Section C

Read the following information and look at questions 22–33. You're going to hear an interview with Sally, a book designer. Listen, and complete the information for questions 22–33. You can write a maximum of six words in any one gap although sometimes you need to write only one word. When you have finished, you'll hear the piece again.

NOTES: A 'raw manuscript' is a book received from an author in typewritten or some other form.
A 'high priority title' is a book which is at the top of a publisher's list of future publications.

Sally is given a brief for any manuscript she is working on. This tells her (22) ....
The main aim of her work is to create a book which (23) ....
Sally decided to do an A-level in art because she thought it would be (24) ....
When Sally started at university she intended to specialise in (25) .... and (26) ....
The main thing she really likes about being a designer is (27) ....
Just one of the problems that Sally has to solve is making lots of bits of material (28) ....
Sally doesn't like receiving artwork in the post because she is afraid she may have (29) ....
(30) .... Sally will be away on holiday, so now she is working long hours to (31) ....
Her situation is made more stressful by other people who (32) ....
Despite the fact that it is quite stressful, Sally enjoys her job because she finds it exciting creating a book that (33) ....

Section D

Read the following information and look at questions 34-40. You are going to hear a number of different people talking about their favourite films. You must decide who is talking and what kind of film they are talking about. For each extract (questions 34-40) write the letter of one person and one kind of film The first one (34) has been done for you as an example. There are more people and kinds of films on the lists than you will hear on tape. When you have finished, you'll hear the piece again.

34 .Ca.....	**A** teacher	**a** Western
35	**B** actor	**b** love story
36	**C** police officer	**c** musical
37	**D** schoolchild	**d** cartoon
38	**E** film producer	**e** detective story
39	**F** musician	**f** thriller
40	**G** film critic	**g** comedy
	H doctor	**h** science fiction
	I writer	**i** war adventure

PAPER 5 : SPEAKING

Time: Approx. 15 minutes

Work in pairs throughout this Speaking Paper.

Phase A

Even though you might know each other well, do the following:

- Introduce yourself to your partner.
- Tell your partner about your plans and ambitions for the next few years.
- Ask your partner questions to find out more about his or her future plans with regard to **a**) work and study, and **b**) family and relationships.

Phase B

Student A: look at page 66 and describe what you can see there.

Student B: look at these two sentences and explain how they relate to what your partner described.

YOU NEVER KNOW WHO YOU'LL MEET
ON THE PAGES
OF THE NATIONAL GEOGRAPHIC MAGAZINE

AN ENGLISH COUNTRY COTTAGE
(with constant supply of running water)

Phase C

You agree to take part in this research. Discuss the questions your teacher puts to you.

Please help us in our research into Memory.

Come to the Psychology Department at 4 p.m.

Phase D [Teacher]

Exam Three

PAPER 1: READING

Time: 1 hour

1 Questions 1–11. Below and opposite are the first thirteen paragraphs of an article in which the (male) writer discusses the issue of women's equality. Read it in order to answer these questions. For each question write the paragraph letter(s), **A**, **B**, **C**, **AD**, **GK**, etc.

In which paragraph does the writer introduce the point about the success of women as heads of state? 1 ...
Which paragraph concludes that we are are all of equal worth? 2 ...
Which paragraph attacks the argument that women have been too busy at home to become great artists? 3 ...
Which paragraph first states that women's abilities have nothing to do with women's rights? 4 ...
In which paragraph does he try to put himself firmly on the side of women? 5 ...
Which paragraph points out that women have always had the chance to perform music in public? 6 ...
Which two paragraphs acknowldege the success women have had in one particular art form? 7 ...
8 ...
Which paragraph examines women's lack of success as playwrights? 9 ...
Which paragraph points out that, if anything, some girls had a better cultural education than boys? 10 ...
Which paragraph asserts that we are not all equally gifted? 11 ...

WOMEN'S RIGHTS AND WRONGS

A The chief reason why George Orwell was so incensed by socialist drivel and attacked it with such ferocity is that he was a socialist himself. Few things are so enraging as hearing bad arguments and false claims put forward for a cause you passionately believe in.

B For me the equivalent example is women's rights. I believe in them wholeheartedly, but most of the familiar arguments put forward for them by feminists are either bad arguments or irrelevant to the case. And they do the cause itself, which is right and just, no good.

C What leads so many into this morass of bad argument is an initial claim which they mistakenly feel compelled to make, a claim which even if it is true has no relevance. It is the claim that women are in all important respects as capable as men. Well may they be, but it has nothing to do with their right to legal and social equality.

D When the Rights of Man were proclaimed in the 18th century it never occurred to anyone to base this call on the assertions that all men were of equal intelligence or equal ability, or equal potential. Very obviously they are not. A few men are creative but nearly all are not; some are brilliant organisers while some are hopeless; some are intelligent and some are foolish; some are strong and some are weak. These are facts that are self-evident to everyone.

E If the argument for social equality among men had rested on a denial of them, it would have been a non-starter. The fundamental fact-value distinction is of the essence here. The case for equal rights and equal opportunities is not built on factual claims at all, but on moral claims. It rests on the proposition that there is no such thing as an unimportant person. Hero or coward, clever or dull, competent or feckless, all human beings count, matter, are entitled to equal consideration. That is the view.

F Every civilised society nowadays is based on the rule of law combined with the principle of equality before the law. These principles are not negated by the obviously differing aptitudes and intelligence of the individual citizens. So even if it were the case that all men were competent and all women incompetent, women would still have their full right to legal and social equality. This relentless striving to prove that women are as good at this, that and everything else as men, or to provide exculpating reasons when they appear not to be, is entirely beside the point.

G The failure to see this has led feminists into one bad argument after another. Because there has been no great woman composer, painter or playwright they feel compelled to say: 'Women haven't had a chance to do these things.' Historically this is false. For hundreds of years the daughters of so-called good families throughout Europe were taught painting and music as a matter of course, while their brothers were encouraged if anything to follow more 'manly' pursuits such as riding, hunting, archery, fencing and so on.

H If feminists say, 'Ah yes, but women weren't able to have their work publicly exhibited or performed,' that is not true either. Women have been playing musical instruments in public, and some of them have been composing again for hundreds of years.

I Most of Europe's major art galleries include paintings by women going back to previous centuries. The pictures are there: but they are not among the best, and for that reason the names of the artists are little known. But you only have to walk into, say, the National Gallery or the Wallace Collection to see them. Three hundred years ago, during the period of Restoration drama in England, there were many successful women playwrights, some of whose work has recently been reprinted, though it has failed to hold the stage.

J These examples refute another common feminist argument: that it was not possible for women to combine their domestic role with sustained and serious creative work. In any event, their domestic role has not stopped them from writing great novels. Why should it have been compatible with that but not with great symphonies or paintings?

K When feminists fall back on saying, 'But women were not taken seriously, society was not prepared to look on them as weighty or significant figures in the way it was men,' this seems to me the weakest argument of all. Since when has producing original work consisted in doing what other people expected? And in any case it is flatly contradicted by women's achievement as novelists, and by the full public recognition and respect this has won them from the beginning.

L Most obviously of all, this argument is blown sky high by the recurrence throughout so much of recorded history of outstanding women political leaders, and in widely differing societies, from Cleopatra via Boadicea to Queen Elizabeth: or are we being asked to believe that these were not taken seriously by men, and not regarded by society at large as weighty and significant figures?

M The claim that creative ability in music, painting, and the theatre must be distributed randomly between the sexes and therefore that the failure of women to produce great work in any of those fields must be due to inhibiting social factors, falls down on every one of those counts.

2 Questions 12-16. Read this article and then answer the questions opposite.

The months passed. The *shifta* continued their murderous poaching raids until not a single elephant was left alive in Kora; but down in Nairobi the tide was turning. Richard Leakey had taken over the anti-poaching offensive as Kenya's new wild-life and conservation management director; and President Moi, in a dramatic gesture underlining his determination to stamp out the ivory racketeering, publicly burned a pile of confiscated tusks worth £2 million.

The three cubs, meanwhile, were growing fast in Adamson's care. They would not lose their milk teeth until they were 14 months old, but already they accompanied him on walks into the bush, following the dirt roads his brother Terence had built before he died in 1986.

Adamson walked more slowly now, with the aid of a stick; but he could still climb Kora Rocks as he had with all his other lions, with Boy and Christian and Arusha, so many years ago. Those were among his happiest days, and he loved the cubs for giving him a new lease of life.

Friends who visited him in early August were amazed to find the old man in such fine form. He had been poorly after a bout of pneumonia but seemed to be fully recovered. The short rains had come unseasonally early to Kora, bringing a flush of fresh grass and the marvellous smell of slaked earth. The acacia trees burst into blossom and weaver birds had begun to build their raffia nests in the branches. It was the African spring, a time of rebirth and renewal.

Down south in Tsavo, Leakey's men were cracking down on the *shifta*. Thirty poachers had been shot dead and the last of the gangs were on the run. Better still, news reached the Adamson camp that at last, after nearly 20 years of struggle, Kora was to be gazetted as a national park.

Adamson was delighted. Now only one worry continued to nag him. For months he had seen and heard nothing of the wild lions. But then, on August 19th, the strangest thing happened. That evening, after his regular sundowner of White Horse whisky, the entire pride gathered around *Kampi ya Simba*, grunting and roaring all night long. It was, said friends, a magical moment which the old man found inexpressibly moving. He went to bed more contented than he had been for weeks, thrilled that Growe and her pride were still intact. The next day he was shot dead by three Somali bandits as he drove out with his revolver in his hand to rescue his driver, Abdi, and a German guest.

The eulogies poured in from all over the world. Adamson was a warrior for conservation; an ambassador for wild Africa. 'George Adamson put Kenya on the map,' observed Richard Leakey. 'He was a man of incredible character and dedication who died fighting against people who would harm the wildlife he loved so much.'

On September 2 George Adamson was buried at Kora as he had wished, beside the grave of his brother Terence and that of Supercub, one of their favourite lions. A simple cairn marks the spot.

12 Which of these statements accurately describes the situation at the opening of the extract?

A Poaching had been given a boost by the country's president.
B Mr Leakey had stopped the slaughter of elephants in the north.
C The situation was grave in the north but even worse in the south.
D There were signs that the anti-poaching movement was gaining ground.

13 In August of that year, what was Adamson's state of mind or health?

A He was suffering from pneumonia.
B He had been rejuvenated by the young lions.
C He was restricted in his movements.
D He knew he was about to die.

14 We learn that the short rains in Kenya normally come

A in the African winter.
B in June.
C later in the African spring.
D when the grass has grown.

15 Which gave Adamson the greatest pleasure?

A The fact that the poachers had been defeated.
B The rebirth of nature that spring brought.
C Official recognition for his nature reserve.
D He had recovered from his bout of pneumonia.

16 The irony of Adamson's death is that he died

A trying to help his enemies.
B when he had finally won his struggle.
C at the hands of the pride that he so loved.
D for reasons unconnected with wildlife.

3 **Read these extracts from letters to a newspaper in response to one by a Mr B Cassatt. Then answer the questions opposite.**

a Mr B Cassatt's point is well-made. In the case of a disaster such as the drowning of hundreds under an upturned ferry or the crushing of nearly a hundred against stadium fences, surely the most appropriate response by the media is a dignified silence. Whether commuters trapped in an underground blaze or innocent passengers blown out of the sky over Scotland, these people deserve to be better served than they are at present by press and television. Their bereaved relatives indeed deserve better than to have cameras and microphones thrust at them until they can no longer hold back tears.

b Mr Cassatt wrote of the multiple deaths with which we have been beset of late and suggested that, as he puts it, the individual 'martyr to fog' on our motorways is all but ignored because he is not one of a hundred. In fact his memory is short. Television — and perhaps the viewer — seems to need the individual even to crystalise a multiple horror. Cambodia for many people is a single photograph of a napalm-covered child, while nearer to home the young, newly-wed captain of the Thames boat disaster, for reporter and reported to, became the symbol of the tragedy. We can hardly be said to ignore or belittle individual death; in such instances we almost glorify it.

c The flames have barely been extinguished when the recriminations start, the blame apportioned. And it is the press that inflames the situation with speculation, interviewing, pressurising people not in possession of all the fact into an incautious word which will allow them to point the finger. We meanwhile share their bated breath as we wait for the latest casualty figures in the next bulletin or edition.

d As Mr Cassatt points out, quite clearly heads have to roll whenever such a disaster strikes, if only for the man in the street's peace of mind.

e ... what he calls an undignified scrabble for money. Mr Cassatt forgets that in some cases relatives of victims have to wait upward of three years before their claims are settled. It is not avarice. It is not revenge. It is justice they seek.

f As someone not similarly bereaved, Mr Cassatt obviously does not appreciate the need such people feel to mark their tragedy and remember a fifth or tenth anniversary of their loss. Moreover, to say this is TV making cheap capital out of people's misery does him no credit. Such things should not be forgotten.

g Perhaps the crux of the matter — and I feel this point has eluded Mr Cassatt — is that we have simply too much news. Just as for days before an international summit meeting we are swamped with speculation, 'expert comment' and 'informed opinion' to the point of tedium, so after a disaster every angle is explored and no stone left unturned in an attempt to extract every last newsworthy word out of any given drama.

h His comments about Chernobyl and Armenia overlook the fact that tragedies will always strike harder when they affect people one can easily relate to; he should not castigate the average Englishman for becoming sentimental about his fellow countrymen's football fans or holidaymakers.

Questions 17–24. Which of these points did Mr Cassatt probably make in his letter to the newspaper?
Tick (√) if you think he did. If you don't think he did, put a dash ' — '.

TV cameras intrude too much on private grief.	17 ...
Compensation to victims' relatives should be made more quickly.	18 ...
People responsible for disasters should not continue in their position.	19 ...
We are prepared to care about an individual's plight more than a large number of victims.	20 ...
It is important that anniversaries of tragedies are marked and remembered.	21 ...
'International' disasters are often more serious than ones in Britain.	22 ...
We could do with less media coverage of everything that is happening.	23 ...
Why is TV so fond of '10 years ago today, 200 people lost their lives'?	24 ...

Questions 25–29. Which of the extracts a–h can be summarised like this?
Write the letter against the question number.

The nearer a disaster happens, the more involved one will feel.	25 ...
Media coverage of world events has reached saturation point.	26 ...
Viewers respond more readily to pictures of individual misery than the concept of multiple deaths.	27 ...
The media are too quick to draw conclusions.	28 ...
The bereaved should not be blamed for claiming financial compensation.	29 ...

4 Questions 30–40. Read these book reviews and answer the questions opposite by writing the appropriate letter of the book (**A, B, C, D** or **E**).

GRIM TALES

Short Stories

Ann Thwaite

Malcolm Bradbury has defined the British short story as 'an idea that might have been a novel but wasn't a big enough idea'. There is some feeling, certainly, that short stories for children don't sell, unless they are fairy tales, ghost or pony stories. Rather than collections of ideas that might have been novels if they had been bigger, here we have a number of books — with the stories in each linked to one another — that might have been novels if they had been given a more complex structure.

A The most challenging is undoubtedly **The Bus People**, by Rachel Anderson (Oxford, £6.95). The publishers had a problem with the jacket: how does one illustrate a book about the mentally handicapped? The fine drawings by Maggie Palmer suggest it is for young children. It is not.

Rachel Anderson faces up to everything, 'the fits and the shrieks, the nodding heads and the rolling eyes'. There is a 15-year-old Downs Syndrome girl, not allowed to be a bridesmaid at her beloved sister's wedding. There's a boy confined to a wheelchair, dribbling, incontinent, at the onset of puberty, smothered by his mother's unintelligent love; a pretty autistic girl, a small black spastic boy, another boy brain-damaged in a bicycle accident.

The telling is so vivid and unsentimental that the reader — adult, teenage, top primary perhaps — will weep for all the damaged children in the world, and resolve 'to accept people as they are, rather than for what they can do'. A remarkable book, it could be read aloud most effectively by teachers who accept its challenges; its lessons are serious and subtle.

B **Timepieces** by David Leney, illustrated by Tony Kerins (Dent £8.95), is for primary school children. Leney himself is head of a village school in Suffolk and he writes entertainingly of what he knows. There's one story for each month of the year, culminating in a June school outing to London, when the children start on their packed lunches before they even get to Liverpool Street.

The children are never stereotyped, they talk as children do talk. This is fiction holding up mirrors, rather than opening windows, and worth several hours of any junior's time.

C **Then the Zeppelins Came** by Dorothy Horgan (Oxford, £7.95), is less satisfactory. The stories about prim Emily and daring Lizzie start in 1909, when they are Mixed Infants, and end with them grown up, celebrating the end of the first world war. Horgan is apparently basing her stories on family history, but the social detail often seems strange. It seems unlikely that someone who was 'very well-off with a large estate in Cork' should have worked as a governess in Belgium and attended the At Homes of someone who had once been 'in service'. No doubt she did in real life, but art has to be more convincing than real life.

D Michael Rosen in **The Deadman Tapes** (Deutsch Adlib, £3.50) has a brilliantly simple and effective idea. Paul Deadman has found in the attic of his new house a series of eight tapes, recorded anonymously by a group of young people. What they say is set as verse, which it really isn't. It is talk, and extremely readable.

The voices speak of all those things the young are most concerned about — sex, violence, racism, human relationships of every sort. They will have to try to work out, just as Paul Deadman does, who is talking and what is going on. 'I know them all now,' he says, 'I know these people I've never met.' So will the reader.

E In **Dark Toys and Consumer Goods** (Macmillan, £6.95), Laurence Staig tells some disturbing cautionary 'tales of a consumer society'. The stories are set in a grim future, where you can only watch TV if you have an 'addiction-free registration number'. Everyone is labelled. The mindless disruptives are in the Riot Zone, while the majority are mindlessly consuming in the Happy Sterling Shopping Mall. Superficially the stories are easy reading (lots of short paragraphs, dialogue, buzz words) but they are at times quite difficult. It is an ugly book with some important messages.

Downs Syndrome: a medical condition in which a baby is born with 47 rather than 46 chromosomes in each cell. This results in a characteristic appearance (a round flat face and a short thickset body) and some degree of mental handicap. Despite their handicap, however, Downs Syndrome children are often happy and well adjusted.
Liverpool Street: this is Liverpool Street Station in London.
Zeppelin: a rigid, cigar-shaped dirigible airship used for transatlantic voyages (from 1928) and, in the First World War, by the Germans for bombing raids [named after Graf Ferdinand von Zeppelin (1838–1917)]

Which of the books

- is aiming at the youngest readership? 30 ...
- treats the sensitive issue of the disabled? 31 ...
- has a futuristic theme? 32 ...
- will have the most profound effect on the reader emotionally? 33 ...
- was obviously written from first hand experience? 34 ...
- might be seen as a kind of warning? 35 ...
- has an element of mystery? 36 ...
- is factually unconvincing? 37 ...
- has rather misleading artwork? 38 ...
- has twelve separate stories? 39 ...
- deals with a number of adult subjects? 40 ...

PAPER 2: WRITING

Time: 2 hours

Section A

You work in a publishing office which produces a monthly magazine. Your superior, David Blackwell (D.B.), is away in the U.S.A. You have been away for two days yourself and return to the office to find a note from a colleague who is going on holiday for two weeks, and a certain amount of correspondence. Below you see his note, a telex, and the closing lines of a threatening letter. Write a full report to D.B., explaining the situation, saying what you propose to do about the crisis and/or asking him for any directives necessary. You should write about 250 words.

Sorry to leave you with so many headaches; don't know what DB is going to say! Jackson's not placing their ads with us is really going to hit revenue. And there's more!
Janet's leaving and won't be writing features for the next issue. The printers say that if we want full colour in future, we're going to have to pay half as much again. And, as you'll see from the letter, we've got trouble from Italy following last month's article on foreign banks.

The first thing to do is inform DB of the way things are. I should write him a full report, making excuses where you can, tell him what you propose to do in some cases, and ask him what he wants done in others. His fax number in N.Y. is ..... I shouldn't mention the fire in the photocopying room, but perhaps he ought to know about the cleaners' 15% pay increase demand.

See you in a fortnight.

REGRET TO INFORM YOU WE ARE WITHDRAWING OUR ADVERTISING AS FROM LAST ISSUE STOP POOR CIRCULATION FIGURES IN FIRST QUARTER RENDER OUR PARTICIPATION FINANCIALLY UNVIABLE STOP BEST WISHES FOR FUTURE OF MAGAZINE STOP JACKSON AND SONS STOP

We might be able to get Clarion Carpets to fill the space !!!

Unless we receive a full apology in your next issue, we shall be obliged to put the matter into the hands of our solicitors.

Yours faithfully,

Luigi Mancini

Luigi Mancini, Director

GREY-HAIRED AND WRINKLED? WHY NOT BE A POP STAR?

POP MUSIC is exactly not what it used to be. Or it is? A list of successful (33).......
major world tours by groups and artists over the past few years includes (34).......
names such as The Rolling Stones, Tina Turner, Bob Dylan and Paul
McCartney, some of whom will not see fifty again, forty let alone. Pop (35).......
music for the young by the young?

Tina Turner still struts her stuff regularly while The Stones and
McCartney, the most famous products of the sixties, both have had (36).......
highly successful albums, singles and videos this year. Nearer fifty than
forty now, though you hardly would think it from his appearance, (37).......
baby-faced Cliff Richard just has recorded his 110th British Top Forty hit (38).......
and Freddy Mercury of 'Queen' gives also performances unthinkable for a (39).......
man of his age thirty years ago. In America, The Beach Boys, Chubby
Checker and Paul Simon, to name but a few, are all still active in the
world of popular music. It doesn't probably get reflected in the singles (40).......
charts, it's true, but be that as it may, there can be little doubt that rock (41).......
stars are getting older or are being rather allowed to go on longer before (42).......
being put to grass out. Were there to be an all-generation popularity poll, (43).......
it is likely that a number of the top ten polled would be the wrong side
of forty-five. Not since the forties that has been true. (44).......

Perhaps people prefer to forget the age of some of their ageing heroes.
Had Blondie's Debbie Harry not recently made public her real age, few (45).......
would have guessed she is nearing fifty. Do people look at Mick Jagger's
lips and forget generously the laughter lines? To think there was a time not (46).......
so long ago when any performer approaching thirty automatically was (47).......
considered a has-been! And yet, as everyone knows, the weekly singles'
charts are more often than not dominated by extremely youthful singers
and groups. Some record-producers don't still seem to realise that there (48).......
is a record-buying public beyond that of the little nice schoolgirl. (49).......

4 At a recent music club concert, you carelessly turned over two pages instead of one during a visiting pianist's recital. As it was a good friend, your embarrassment was not too great, but you wrote a short note to apologise. By an awful coincidence something similar happened yesterday evening, but this time the player was a well-known professional pianist. You wrote a slightly longer letter to him with the same message but more carefully chosen words. Complete the two letters in the spaces below.

Do not write more than two words in any one space. The first one has been done for you as an example.

Dear Sonja,

Thanks again for the ...(50)... performance you gave at our show last night. I must say you were in great form

The people ...(51)... every minute of it; everybody was coming up at the end and saying how much they ...(52)... it.

I'm ever ...(53)... about my little gaffe. I can imagine how annoying it was. Believe me, it's the ...(54)... I've ever done it and I've still ...(55)... how it happened.

I don't suppose there's ...(56)... of you being down here for ...(57)... but I hope it ...(58)... too long before we can get you back. I promise I'll ...(59)... someone else to turn the pages!

Kind regards and thanks again.

Yours,

Dear Mr Sikorski,

I ...(60)... to thank you again for the thrilling performance you gave at our gala evening yesterday. The ...(61)... was enchanted and we were swamped afterwards with praise for having invited you.

I really must ...(62)... for my inexcusable lapse. I appreciate how off-putting it must have been for you and ...(63)... you I am not in the ...(64)... doing such things. I am still at a ...(65)... to explain how it happened

I realise that there is ...(66)... of you being available for another concert in the near future, but I hope that one day we might be able to invite you again and have the honour and pleasure of your playing once more.

Thank you again for a ...(67)... performance.

Yours sincerely,

50 ..*really fantastic*........

51 ....

52 ....

53 ....

54 ....

55 ....

56 ....

57 ....

58 ....

59 ....

60 ....

61 ....

62 ....

63 ....

64 ....

65 ....

66 ....

67 ....

EXAM ONE: Paper 5 Speaking — Phase B

Student 1: Study this photo and be prepared to describe it to your partner. After a minute your partner will describe his or her photo to you.

EXAM THREE: Paper 5 Speaking — Phase B

Student 1:

1 Look at these photos. Describe each room in as much detail as possible to your partner.

2 Look at the photos on page 72. Discuss which of these people is most likely to live in the four rooms you have photos of. Look at each other's pictures now, too.

EXAM TWO: Paper 5 Speaking — Phase B

Student 1: Study these photos and describe them to your partner. He or she will then try to match them with slogans.

Section C

5 Choose the best phrases or sentences from those given below to fill the blanks in this text. Write one letter **(A–J)** in each of the numbered spaces.

NOTE: Three of the suggested answers do not fit at all.

PHOTOGRAPHING SPORT

For many people, taking pictures of their favourite sports is the ideal way to mix two hobbies. Any sport can be photographed. But some sports — notably motor racing — favour the professional with the press passes. (68) ...., someone with a telephoto lens can often get as good a picture from the terraces as someone on the sidelines with the same lens. A single-minded attitude is as necessary as quick reflexes (69) .... that are anything more than run-of-the-mill records. Above all, you have to prepare yourself and be prepared.

This means: (70) .... Obviously, the type of event you attend, and the type of picture you hope to achieve will dictate what equipment you need. Long focal length lenses are practical, particularly when you are likely to be distanced from the action, but, clearly, your equipment must serve your aims. Some top sports photographers make almost as much use of wide-angle lenses as telephotos.

(71) .... Being familiar with the movements of participants is half the battle with peak-of-action photography where anticipation is critical. (72) .... , don't fire a frame until you have accustomed yourself to the pace and rhythm of play or performance.

(73) .... Before the event, try to get access, then wander round, think about the direction of light and look for the best vantage points. Ideally, these will provide a good view of places where the drama is bound to occur, such as the crest of a hill in a motocross circuit or a bend at a track event.

Always check with the organisers (74) .... Some venues issue passes to photographers. Many organisers do not permit flash, and those concerned with golf, for example, frown on motor-drives.

A if you are new to the sport

B if you enjoy sport

C it helps to know a sport

D that it's permissible to take photographs

E the best photos are often taken by amateurs

F keep equipment to a minimum

G it also helps to know the terrain

H as any seasoned photographer will tell you

I it helps to have plenty of film

J if you are to come away with sports pictures

6 Look at the encyclopedia notes below about Hong Kong. You have been asked to write the information out in full sentences for a tourist information sheet. You may add words and change the form of words where necessary. Look carefully at these two examples:

H.K. situated S.E. coast China

Hong Kong is situated on the south-east coast of China.

total area: 1,031 sq.kilometres; pop (est. 1981) 5,000,000

It has a total area of 1,031 sqare kilometres and in 1981 had an estimated population of five million.

(75) cap. Victoria (pop. 1,200,000), located south side of marvellous harbour

(76) ave. temp. 15° C (Feb) 28° C (July)

(77) rainy season: May-Sept, inc. typhoons; ave. 216 cm rain per an.

(78) main crops: rice, veg. fruit

(79) industr: textiles,shipbldng,iron & steel, aircraft engin., elec. equip., light manuf.

(80) industr. development rapid since World War 2

(81) H.K. ceded to Brit. by Chinese in 1898; 99-year lease due to expire 1997

(82) Over 1m. refugees from mainland Ch. in past 40 yrs.

(75) ______________________________

(76) ______________________________

(77) ______________________________

(78) ______________________________

(79) ______________________________

(80) ______________________________

(81) ______________________________

(82) ______________________________

PAPER 4 : LISTENING

Time: Approx. 45 minutes

In this test you will hear four extracts of spoken English and you will be given time to choose your answers to the questions or to write answers. Before you listen to each extract, read the questions carefully. Read or look again while you are listening and choose **A**, **B**, **C** or **D**, complete the sentences, or do whatever you are asked to do. In **Section A**, **Section C** and **Section D** check your answers while you are listening for the second time. In **Section B** you will only hear the piece once.

Section A

Read the following information and look at questions 1–12. You're going to hear the introductory talk at a conference on Healthy Living. There are some changes to the published programme. Listen to the first part of Mrs Baker's talk and, for questions 1–12, mark the changes on the programme, as in the example, which changes 'Professor D Unwin' to 'Mrs Baker'. If you think no change is needed for a numbered item, do nothing. When you have finished, you'll hear the piece again.

HEALTHY LIVING CONFERENCE

PROGRAMME FOR SATURDAY OCTOBER 24

09.00 - 09.15	Introductory Welcome	Main Hall	Mrs Celia Baker
09.15 - 10.00	Pulses and Cereals	Lecture Room 1	Ms Kathy Spark
09.15 - 10.00	Caring for your Heart	Lecture Room 2	Dr Spencer Hall
10.15 - 11.00	**1** The Vegan Way	Room 3C	*Mrs Baker* ~~Prof D Unwin~~
10.15 - 11.00	Nouvelle Cuisine	Lecture Room 3	M Marcel Roux
11.00 - 11.30	Coffee/Tea	Refectory	
11.30 - 12.15	Yoga Workshop	**2** Room 2A	**3** Mr & Mrs A Smythe
11.30 - 12.15	Subtracting Additives	Lecture Room 2	Mrs Eva Hoddinot
12.30 - 13.15	Herbal Remedies	Lecture Room 1	Mrs Y Thompson
12.30 - 13.15	Dietary Supplements	**4** Lecture Room 3	Mr Larry Blake
13.15 - 14.15	Lunch	Dining Hall	
14.30 - 15.30	A Healthy Pregnancy	Lecture Room 1	Dr W Willis
14.30 - 15.30	**5** What's what in Keep-Fit	Lecture Room 2	Mr B Hodgeson
15.45 - 16.45	Childhood Illnesses	Main Hall	Ms Mary Watkins
6 15.45 - 16.45	**7** t.b.a.	Room 4	**8** t.b.a.
	9 Dinner and Entertainment	**10** Queen's Hotel, Hove	
		11 Coach leaves from College Gates at 18.00	
		12 Return approx. 23.00	

Section B

Read the following information and look at questions 13-23. You're going to hear a recorded message left on the answering machine of a large mail order company. As you listen, look at the sentences 13-23 and put a line through the option a) or b) which is *not* true. The first one has been done for you. Listen very carefully: you will hear the message only once.

13 Mr Finch a) regrets the fact that he is speaking to an answering machine.
b) ~~is relieved~~

14 He mentions the time of day because he a) thinks someone should be there.
b) realises it's rather late.

15 The chairs arrived a) soon after being ordered.
b) a long time

16 Mr Finch a) accepts the blame for the appearance of the assembled chair.
b) doesn't accept

17 He a) paid for the return postage himself.
b) didn't pay

18 His comment about records is a) an insult.
b) a compliment.

19 The way he uses the word *advantages* implies a) benefits.
b) inconvenience.

20 Court action was first threatened because a) the chairs were sub-standard.
b) the chairs were not paid for.

21 When he says *great*, he means a) wonderful.
b) terrible.

22 The chairs are now a) with Mr Finch.
b) on their way back to the company.

23 Between six and seven is a time for the company a) to avoid.
b) to arrange a visit.

Section C

Read the following information and the descriptions of people (**A–H**) at the top of page 71. For a not-too-serious item in a radio magazine programme, a number of people were asked how they deal with their boiled eggs for breakfast; do they start at the pointed end or the round end, do they smash the egg, slice off the top or peel off the shell, etc? Apparently this may be a clue to their character! You're going to hear eight people giving their comments. Task 1: Questions 24–31. Match the speakers with the descriptions by writing the letters **A**, **B**, **C**, etc. as appropriate against the speaker numbers. The first one (item 24) has been done for you.

24 .B.	**A**	someone who has no fixed pattern
25	**B**	someone who doesn't eat eggs
26	**C**	someone who turns their eggshell upside down afterwards
27	**D**	someone who always starts at the pointed end
28	**E**	someone who dips bread into the egg
29	**F**	someone who shows impatience with the interviewer
30	**G**	someone who doesn't like boiled eggs at all
31	**H**	someone who is interested in the psychological aspect

Read the following information.Task 2: questions 32–38.You're going to hear some of the interviews again. On the left are seven ways of treating a boiled egg (numbered 32–38); on the right, the psychologist's analysis of attitudes towards money (labelled **A–G**). As you listen, match the eating habits (on the left) with the attitudes towards money (on the right). Write the appropriate letter against each item number. One has been done for you already.

Pointed end	32 .D.	**A**	occasionally impulsive buying silly luxuries
Rounded end	33	**B**	extremely cautious, saves, doesn't spend
Slicing	34	**C**	spends for the fun of it, extremely generous
Smashing	35	**D**	takes risks, gambles
Peeling	36	**E**	worries about money, debts etc.
Dipping	37	**F**	well-balanced attitude to money
Turning eggshell upside down ...	38	**G**	finds money boring

Section D

Read the following information and the descriptions of people below. You're going to hear nine people talking about the police. Study the list of people and, as you listen, for questions 39–47 write the letter of the speaker **(A, B, C,** etc.) beside the number of the person you hear talking. There are more people in the list than there are speakers on tape. When you have finished, you'll hear the piece again.

39 ...
40 ...
41 ...
42 ...
43 ...
44 ...
45 ...
46 ...
47 ...

A A chief inspector
B Someone worried about the police
C A young police constable
D A policewoman
E An advertising 'voice-over'
F An 'anti-police' politician
G A supporter of the police
H A criminal
I A magistrate or judge
J A militant student
K A newsreader

PAPER 5 : SPEAKING

Time: Approx. 15 minutes

Work in pairs throughout this Speaking Paper.

Phase A

Even though you might know each other well, do the following:

- Introduce yourself to your partner.
- Tell your partner something about your background — your family, your education, and so on.
- Ask your partner some questions to find out more about what he or she has done in the last five years.

Phase B

Student 1: turn to page 65. **Student 2**: turn to page 99.

Do not look at each other's material.

Phase C

Look at these four photos and discuss the questions your teacher asks you.

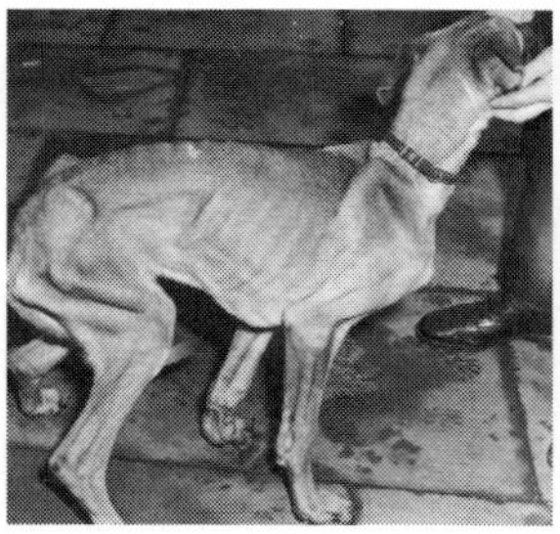

Phase D [Teacher]

Exam Four

PAPER 1: READING

Time: 1 hour

1 Questions 1–4. Read this passage and answer the multiple-choice questions. Choose the one answer or sentence completion which you think fits best — **A, B, C** or **D**.

What if ... ?

Have you ever wondered what might have happened if President Kennedy had survived the assassination of 1963? Pure speculation, you'll say. Kennedy *was* assassinated in Dallas, Texas, on 22nd November, 1963. And that's an end to it. The rest is recent history.

But what if he had survived? It's the stuff novels are made of. And in 1988 the American film studio executive turned lawyer turned novelist George Bernau published a novel on just this theme. The book is called *Promises to Keep*, and is described in the cover blurb as 'the most compelling and explosive thriller since *The Day of the Jackal*'. The book is an example of what has come to be known as 'faction' — fiction based on (or should it be, in?) fact. And it is a very good example at that.

The 'New York Newsday' had this to say about it: 'Most "what if" novels are failures. Almost surprisingly, Bernau's succeeds. He has done his homework and he makes all the complexities of the White House power politics and political machinations feel authentic. He weaves together two plots, political and conspiratorial ... both have the tensions of high drama ... *Promises to Keep* is gripping — the kind of novel that forces the reader to keep turning the page till the end.' And so it is: 800-plus pages it might be, but once I got into it, I couldn't put it down.

In reality, as we all know, John F. Kennedy never regained consciousness after he was shot in the cavalcade through Dallas: in this novel, his life is saved — and the plot unfolds from there.

The book set me thinking, not specifically about the Kennedy assassination, although of course it did that, but about the possibilities of the 'What if ...?' novel as a genre. Naturally I've a few ideas of my own to keep me busy for a few years, but if you see yourself as a budding novelist, and would like to try your hand at one, how about these as starters: What if the Russian Revolution in 1917 had failed? And what if John Logie Baird had never invented television?

1 What kind of a book is *Promises to Keep?*
- **A** An investigation into Kennedy's assassination.
- **B** An American horror novel.
- **C** A biography of Kennedy.
- **D** A thriller based on fact.

2 The writer of this passage finished the book even though
- **A** he rarely reads books that long.
- **B** it was about the Kennedy family.
- **C** he hates what he calls 'faction'.
- **D** he didn't believe the 'New York Newsday' review.

3 What, in *Promises to Keep,* is different from the events in history?
- **A** The President is assassinated in the White House.
- **B** Kenndey survives.
- **C** Kennedy and his wife are both shot.
- **D** The assassination is the result of a conspiracy.

4 The writer makes a few suggestions at the end of the passage.For whom?
- **A** Established authors.
- **B** Students of literature.
- **C** Writers of 'What if ...?' novels.
- **D** People who'd like to be novelists.

2 Questions 5–14. People speculate about the oddest things. The letters opposite all appeared in a British newspaper early in January 1990. Decades have often been given names — the 1960s were the 'Swinging Sixties', for example. And the 1890s are now known in Britain as the 'Naughty Nineties'. Read the letters to the editor and match them with the names below.

Which of the possible names for the Nineteen–nineties (below) did the different correspondents suggest? Write the letters (**a**, **b**, **c**, etc) against the appropriate numbers of the letters to the editor. There are more suggested titles for the 1990s than Letters to the Editor.

a	The Nasty Nineties	5 ...
b	The Nutritious Nineties	6 ...
c	The Nicer Nineties	7 ...
d	The Neighbourly Nineties	8 ...
e	The 'Never Pay' Nineties	9 ...
f	The Nosey Nineties	10 ...
g	The Noble Nineties	11 ...
h	The Natural Nineties	12 ...
i	The Nervous Nineties	13 ...
j	The Non-Nuclear Nineties	14 ...
k	The Noisy Nineties	
l	The Notorious Nineties	
m	The Nutty Nineties	

LETTERS TO THE EDITOR

January 9, 1990

Naming the Nineties

5 Sir,
I suggest that your correspondent on 1st January is a little premature in even thinking of a suitable epithet for the 1990s. However, now that the subject has been broached, who am I to hold back? With it becoming increasingly difficult to find peace and quiet in our modern world, I wonder if we shall look back on them sadly as .... ?
Yours sincerely,

6 Sir,
We are entering exciting, but turbulent and worrying times. I think .... might not be a bad description for them.
Yours faithfully,

7 Dear Sir,
If the environmental movement continues to gather momentum, as I feel sure it must and will, it is more than possible that the new age will be known in future as ....
Yours hopefully,

8 Sir,
In spite of the growth of the human rights and civil liberties movements in the 70s and 80s, people in all countries are still subject to invasion of their privacy, mostly perhaps in the West by inquisitive so-called 'civil servants'. If the interest of the authorities in people's private lives were to increase in the next ten years, then might they not be called ....?
Yours privately(!),

9 Dear Sir,
In view of the increasing bonds and the crumbling barriers between so many countries, might the term .... be appropriate?
Yours sincerely,

10 Sir,
I pray we have seen the last of the atomic bomb, and perhaps we can also look forward to the end of atomic energy. If so, then they will surely be described in future history books as ....
Yours truly,

11 Sir,
I have to admit that I am a pessimist, and if the predictions of some experts are proved to be correct (changes in climate, international conflicts, etc.) then the next decade is likely to be worse than the rest of the century. I hate to say so, but they could well be ....
Yours faithfully,

12 Dear Sir,
In view of the amazing amounts of debt, both in Britain and in the rest of the world, might not .... be found later to be a suitable description?
Yours sincerely,

13 Sir,
With people becoming more and more concerned with diet, the food they eat, and so on, might we not be embarking on .... ?
Yours faithfully,

14 Sir,
As an eternal optimist, I think the future looks very rosy. So how about .... ? They'll be better than the 1890s, that's for sure!
Yours truly,

3 Questions 15–25. The extracts here all appeared in a book called *Whale Nation* by Heathcote Williams (1988). Read them and answer the questions below. Write the letter of the relevant extract (**a**, **b**, **c**, **d**, etc.) against each question.

In which extract does someone describe being saved by a dolphin? 15 ...

Which extract writer implies that dolphins are more intelligent than men? 16 ...

Extract c suggests that dolphins live to be 100. Which other extract also refers to the age of dolphins? 17 ...

In which extract does the writer suggest that a dolphin's brain may have a greater capacity than man's? 18 ...

One extract actually suggests that dolphins suffer grief and cry. Which? 19 ...

Which two extracts refer to the dolphin's love of music? (Two answers) 20 ...

21 ...

Which extract explains why dolphins are killed with tunafish? 22 ...

Which extract tells us about products from dead dolphins? 23 ...

Which extract describes the deep love a dolpin has for other dolphins? 24 ...

Which extract tells us that there are a number of different kinds of dolphin? 25 ...

a A quarter of a million dolphins are annually killed by the tunafish industry. Dolphins often swim with tunafish and are used as netmarkers, and end up being crushed to death in these nets.

Only in the last twenty-five years have these industries used nets to catch tuna. Before this they used hooks and lines, and the dolphins were safe. But since these were replaced by larger nets, over eight million dolphins have been killed.

[World Marine Life Observers, Newsletter, Essex, 1986]

b Dolphins never abandon their young and if it happens that men catch a young dolphin, adult dolphins go to the extreme to save the imprisoned youngster. They come to the shore, allow the men to strike, hurt and even kill them.

On many occasions it was noticed that dolphins show human sensibilities and tenderness for other dolphins who are in trouble, hurt or sick. If a dolphin dies, others come together and help deliver the dead body to the shore ... Witnesses tell us that on such an occasion, the dolphins weep and lament, showing human sensibility as they mourn the dead dolphin.

Dolphins are extremely sensitive to music and singing, and they very much like young men who are musicians or singers. There is a story, too, of a lark which at the end of the warm season tried to escape the coming cold. By its merry singing it so enchanted a dolphin that the dolphin delivered it over the sea on its back.

[Konrad Gesner (1551-1587), *History of Animals,* Zurich: Franco Furdi, 1586]

c The dolphin is an animal without malice, living to be a hundred years old, loving music and friendly to men.

[Konrad of Megenberg, *Das Buch der Natur,* 1475]

d **D**olphins of a species known as *Tursiops truncatus* crowd by Cape Hatteras, in the St. Lawrence, in huge schools from late autumn to early spring ... As many as a hundred animals could be taken at a single haul. This industry continued into the present century, principally because of a very special kind of oil that can be extracted from the lower jaws of the *Tursiops.*

The oil is taken from the back end of the lower jaw on either side, and, when refined, was once valued as high as twenty dollars a gallon. It is extremely light and perfectly suited for oiling small watches and other delicate instruments. Secondly, the hides of these animals make very fine leather, and the blubber yields other oil of high grade.

[Ivan T. Sanderson, *Follow the Whale,* London: Cassell, 1958]

e **I**n 1945 the wife of a well-known trial attorney residing in Florida was saved from drowning by a dolphin ('Saved by a Porpoise', *Natural History,* LVIII, 1949, 385-386). This woman had stepped into a sea with a strong undertow and was immediately dragged under. Just before losing consciousness, she remembers hoping that someone would push her ashore. 'With that, someone gave me a tremendous shove, and I landed on the beach, face down, too exhausted to turn over ... when I did, no one was near, but in the water almost eighteen feet out a porpoise was leaping around, and a few feet beyond him another large fish was also leaping.'

In this case the porpoise was almost certainly a dolphin and the large fish a fishtail shark. A man who had observed the events from the other side of a fence told the rescued woman that this was the second time he had seen a drowning person saved by a 'porpoise'.

[Winthrop N. Kellogg, *Porpoises and Sonar,* Chicago: University of Chicago Press, 1961]

f **D**olphin societies are extraordinarily complex, and up to ten generations co-exist at one time. If that were the case with man, Leonardo da Vinci, Faraday, and Einstein would still be alive ... Could not the dolphin's brain contain an amount of information comparable in volume to the thousands of tons of books in our libraries?

[Senator Hubert Humphrey, quoting the Russian delphinologist, Yabalkov, at the 1970 U.S. Senate hearings on the Marine Mammal Protection Act.]

g **N**o sooner does man discover intelligence than he tries to involve it in his own stupidity.

[Jacques Cousteau, *The Living Sea,* New York: Harper and Row, 1963]

4 Questions 26–35. Read the article carefully. Which points does the writer make? Tick (√) if you think she does. Put a dash '—' if you don't think she makes the point.

You are likely to have arguments about who has the best room. 26 ...
People are often completely different when they're on holiday. 27 ...
Quite a lot of couples get on very well together on holiday. 28 ...
The most heated arguments are often about food. 29 ...
When planning a holiday together, couples will often argue about the cost. 30 ...
At least you can sit with people you know on the flight out to your holiday destination. 31 ...
It can work out to be cheaper to share a holiday with another couple. 32 ...
If you want a quiet holiday, don't go with another couple. 33 ...
Bathroom arrangements can be difficult with four sharing. 34 ...
You might find yourselves caught in the middle if the other couple have a marital argument. 35 ...

Questions 36–43. These questions ask you to choose the correct or most appropriate heading for each paragraph numbered **1–8** in the text (below and opposite). **A–L** list possible paragraph headings. Match the correct or most appropriate headings from **A–L** to the paragraphs 1–8. **NOTE**: There is **only one answer** to each question.

Paragraphs

36 ... Paragraph 1
37 ... Paragraph 2
38 ... Paragraph 3
39 ... Paragraph 4
40 ... Paragraph 5
41 ... Paragraph 6
42 ... Paragraph 7
43 ... Paragraph 8

Possible headings

A Those foreign men
B Arguments enough for two
C Sharing linen
D A major advantage
E Go on your own!
F It's all a question of eating
G Job sharing in the villa
H A bag full of taramasalata
I The big question
J The others' habits will get you
K Four's company, two's boredom
L Holidays change people

FOUR'S A CROWD

If the two of you are thinking of sharing your precious hols with that fun couple you thought you knew so well, think again! You could be in for double trouble.

1 Now for the big question of the season. Should you consider doing it with another couple — going on holiday, that is? While an intimate holiday twosome can be fun, you might wonder if a foursome could be more so. You may imagine that your two weeks in Majorca or Margate would be even more memorable if you had another compatible pair along to share your travelling expenses, villa, four-room tent or hotel dining table.

2 Well, of course, taking another couple with you when you go may mean that, on the plane, you won't have to sit next to some stranger who yodels or talks about his open heart surgery. And, if you're on a package, it might mean that this year you won't have to share a hotel dining table with some strange family who like to compare mosquito bites and peel their sunburn.

3 But there are drawbacks to booking a holiday with that nice couple, Julian and Samantha, you met at Greek For Shopping classes, or Joan from work and her boyfriend Bill. True, Julian and Samantha or Joan and Bill may seem perfectly reasonable over your own dinner table. But once on holiday they may change into something ghastly.

4 Once the tropical sun is beating down, the plumbing's playing up, the English newspapers are three days old and the sea's warmer than the lunch, you'll find that cosy couple you thought you knew will show their true colours. Joan will turn into the type who insists on going topless everywhere — yes, even on the local bus to Delphi or on the back of a donkey. Meanwhile, Bill will shout at the natives and wear socks with sandals, then wash his feet in the bidet. Samantha will get stomach trouble, clog up the loo with tissues and dance the tarantella on a table top with a drooling fisherman, causing Julian to bite clean through a cocktail glass.

5 Let's face it, with just two of you on holiday there will be problems enough and disagreements over whether you'll flake out on the beach, climb the cliff face 'because it's there', visit the authentic village in the hills, or just stay in bed soaked in calamine. Multiply these little squabbles by two again, and you can see that you're really in for trouble!

6 Food is the real bone of contention on holiday. With four of you there's always one who wants to go to that little out-of-the-way place that grills snails on charcoal, one who wants to find somewhere that does four courses plus Yorkshire pudding, one who could only manage a sandwich at the beach bar, and one who just wants to be ill!

7 Many a beautiful four-way friendship has ended over dinner in a foreign restaurant. A nervous friend of mine once went on holiday to Greece with a boorish foodie couple who insisted on having taramasalata even though it wasn't a local dish. Eventually the chef made a special effort and presented them with a large plate of vivid pink taramasalata, which the couple then pronounced awful. At which point, my friend, sensitive to the chef's feelings, grabbed a paper napkin, and surreptitiously scooped the offending taramasalata into her hand bag! The beaming waiter took away an empty plate but my friend toured the rest of the Ionian isles with a handbag reeking of cod's roe, and a fleet of seagulls following her wherever she went.

8 If it's peace and quiet and pleasant holiday memories you want, I'd say you and your partner should go it alone. Okay, a table for two doesn't sound such riotous fun as a corner of a taverna for four. But it's better than a two-hour wait for the bathroom and a bagful of fish paste any day!

Marjorca or Margate: the island of Majorca and the British seaside town of Margate are both very popular resorts for British holidaymakers.
Greek for Shopping classes: humorous expression for classes at evening school or college in conversational Greek.
Yorkshire pudding: a thin batter of plain flour, milk, water and salt, baked in an oven in meat fat and popularly eaten in Britain with roast beef.

PAPER 2: WRITING

Time: 2 hours

Section A

The article opposite appeared in a local English newspaper. While some of the information is correct, you are concerned that not only does the article contain incorrect information, but certain vital information (in your view) is not reported at all. You know, because you were at the meeting and made notes yourself.

Compare your notes (below) carefully with the article. Then **write a letter** to the editor of the newspaper criticising the report for its inaccuracies and asking him or her to publish a follow-up article.

You are advised to write approximately 250 words.

- *Meeting attended by at least 500 people*
- *Cost of airport — £38.5 million — was pointed out, this figure likely to rise as the project progressed. Could even be £55 million if project delayed for any reason.*
- *Friends of the Earth and Royal Society for Protection of Birds — gained a lot of support — reason: area designated for new airport site — area of outstanding beauty, home to rare species of birds and other wildlife.*
- *Local villagers — strong objections due to proposed flight paths. Planes would fly straight over their villages — create intolerable noise — reduce value of their property. View supported vigorously by representative of local dairy farmers.*
- *Planners had no real answers to criticisms and doubts about value to local communities.*
- *Local industry all in favour — more light industry — more employment*
- *Question of cost of necessary new roads — planners relying on local authorities to provide new access from all directions — not included in projected costs!*
- *Next meeting in 8 weeks' time.*

New National Airport To Herald In 21st Century

by Ray King Transport Correspondent

THE CENTRAL CITY TOWN HALL was the venue last night for a public meeting about the proposed new international airport. The airport, it was stated, should begin operating in the year 2000.

With the Hall filled to capacity (some 750 people), the Chairman outlined the proposal and suggested that the project would cost in the region of £48.5 million.

'This airport,' said the Chairman, 'will herald in the 21st century and give the country the boost it needs in tourism and international business.'

There was some local support for the scheme, mainly from representatives of local industry, who saw the prospects of more employment. 'We're all in favour', said a spokesman. 'A large new airport will bring with it new light industry, a lot of new service industries, and therefore more jobs for local people.'

Objections to the plan on the grounds of noise and pollution were dismissed by the Chairman as 'exaggerated'. And he added that if local villagers were worried about a reduction in the value of their property, such worries were unfounded.

There was further criticism from other lobbies however. It was pointed out that since the proposal made no mention of access roads, it was felt that local taxpayers would again have to pay.

A further public meeting is planned next month to allow people to air their views about other issues. But things do not look good for the planners of what the Chairman called a major and necessary project 'to herald in the 21st century'.

Section B

Choose **ONE** of the following writing tasks. Your answer should follow exactly the instructions given. You are advised to write approximately 250 words.

1 A colleague recently phoned you from another country to say that he/she will be flying to your country next month and would like to visit you. You said you would love to see him/her and would be happy for him/her to stay with you. However, he/she could not tell you exactly when he/she might be arriving. **Write a letter** confirming your invitation to stay with you and giving clear directions on how to get to your home from the airport using any different forms of transport available. Suggest too that your colleague might like to spend some time with you at your workplace and indicate what he/she might find of interest there.

2 You and the rest of your class have just completed a questionnaire given to you by your teacher as part of a survey on your English learning 'career' over the past two years. At the end of the questionnaire you read this:

> **Thank you for answering the questions in our survey. We would like you finally to add a statement of your own progress in English over the past two years — a kind of 'self-assessment', if you like.**

Write your self-assessment. You may write it as a single narrative report, or as a series of paragraphs with headings such as Reading, Writing, Listening, Speaking, Grammar, Vocabulary, Pronunciation, What I Can Now Do In English, What I Still Can't Do In English, etc.

3 You see this notice in a magazine that you enjoy.

> **What irritates you most in your everyday life?** What do other people do that annoys you? What do you find particularly frustrating when it happens to you? What do you do to help yourself cope with the people and things that irritate you?
> **We are interested in your views.**
> **Write to us** answering these questions as fully as you can, and next month we shall publish an article reporting on what you told us.

You decide to write to the magazine. **Write your contribution.**

4 On some occasion while you were studying abroad last year, you were introduced to the Managing Director of an Anglo-American company who said they were always looking for people like you. You have just completed (or are just about to complete) your studies and would like to work abroad for a year. **Write a letter** to the Managing Director asking if there is a chance you might work in his/her company. Remind him/her of when and where you met, say what you have done since, what qualifications you have acquired (or hope to acquire), and so on.

PAPER 3: ENGLISH IN USE

Time: 1 hour 30 minutes

Section A

1 Complete the following passage by writing the missing words in the spaces provided. Use **only one word** in each space. The first one has been done for you as an example.

People's Interest in their own Language

How do people feel about the way their language is used? My experience is that people fall into three broad categories in their concern over (1) .*how*... their language works. Some (2) .... care less. Many — I think, the majority — care at least some of the time. And some care all of the time. I have tried to write a book (3) .... will be of interest to all three groups. I hope it will be useful to you, (4) .... you are a member of the first group, and have never even dreamed about English usage; or a member of the second, who have lost only the occasional wink of sleep over (5) .... ; or a member of the third, (6) .... regularly have nightmares about it. Readers from all three groups (7) .... at least find the topics familiar. (8) .... all, it was you who asked the questions, provided many of the illustrations, and gave all the answers. It's *your* usage in these pages, not (9) ....

But you can't really care (10) .... something, or take care (11) .... it properly, until you come to know it. (12) .... this book has a serious, underlying purpose, beneath the cartoons — to inform and advise about English usage. I am a firm believer (13) .... the need to talk about the language clearly and accurately, so (14) .... problems of communication can be identified and solved. But I am totally against (15) .... approach which over-intellectualises the subject, or pontificates without reason, (16) .... has happened so often in the past.

2 Read the article below and, in the items opposite, circle the letter next to the word which best fits each space. The first answer has been given as an example.

Business Espionage

Is your telephone bugged? Do you have a 'leaky' boardroom? Does the opposition seem to know what you're up to, what your next product is and when it is coming on stream?

INEXPLICABLE 'LEAKS' of secret or sensitive company information could well be the (17) .... of electronic spy equipment sold openly and legally in every British high street. Nowadays it's not just (18) .... offices and embassies, like the US embassy in Moscow, that have to be 'swept' for bugging devices. The same technology that goes to make the modern calculator or digital watch has been developed to produce bugging devices (19) .... for commercial espionage.

Anyone with a credit card can join the ranks of industrial spies (20) .... by quoting their card number and buying bugging equipment by mail order through (21) .... in magazines. And there are plenty of specialist electronics shops to be found. The 'bugs' are getting more (22) .... and harder to (23) .... , according to professionals in the growing counter-eavesdropping field. Modern micro chip technology (24) .... eavesdropping easy for the industrial spy and there are no (25) .... because eavesdropping itself isn't a criminal (26) .... For the professional, the rewards far (27) .... the risks. Few major corporations are likely to (28) .... they have been duped. First it's too embarrassing and second it might (29) .... others to try their (30) .... at breaking the security screen.

British business is under (31) .... from people prepared to use a whole battery of equipment like long-range (32) .... beamed at boardroom windows from 100 yards away.

17	(**A**) result	**B** answer	**C** purpose	**D** achievement
18	**A** democracy	**B** authority	**C** government	**D** republic
19	**A** abused	**B** wanted	**C** informed	**D** used
20	**A** only	**B** simply	**C** generally	**D** really
21	**A** propaganda	**B** advertising	**C** advice	**D** advertisements
22	**A** educated	**B** sophisticated	**C** clever	**D** complicated
23	**A** detect	**B** find out	**C** discover	**D** uncover
24	**A** allows	**B** entitles	**C** permits	**D** makes
25	**A** expenses	**B** laws	**C** penalties	**D** fees
26	**A** action	**B** thing	**C** offence	**D** crime
27	**A** balance	**B** outweigh	**C** improve	**D** overtake
28	**A** admit	**B** deny	**C** own	**D** confirm
29	**A** encourage	**B** force	**C** drive	**D** push
30	**A** best	**B** hand	**C** hardest	**D** effort
31	**A** threat	**B** promise	**C** danger	**D** orders
32	**A** loudspeakers	**B** lasers	**C** microphones	**D** controls

Section B

3 Read the following text carefully. In many lines, **although not all**, there is a spelling mistake.

Circle each spelling mistake that you find and write the correct spelling at the end of the line. Some lines are correct. Indicate those lines with a tick (√) in the space provided. The first one has been done as an example.

Walking Keeps You Fit

Regarded in the past as inefective for maintaining or	(33)	ineffective
improving fitness, walking has recently come into its own.	(34)	....
The health benefites of exercise less intense than jogging	(35)	....
have been prooved and in the US there are now more than	(36)	....
twice as many fitnes walkers as joggers.	(37)	....
Walking is extremely conveniant and can be social or	(38)	....
solitery depending on your inclination. It can involve the	(39)	....
whole family, with baby riding in a backpack. You can	(40)	....
walk anywhere. There are many journies that can be	(41)	....
completed on foot which are often more pleasant than	(42)	....
travelling on crowded trains and buses. With public foot-	(43)	....
paths and country parks you can also enjoy the countryside.	(44)	....
It is very inexpensive: you will only need a good pair of	(45)	....
walking shoes and waterproof clotheing.	(46)	....
It has been calkulated that walking for, say, 30 minutes	(47)	....
four times a week will demand about the same energy	(48)	....
expenditure as jogging for 20 minutes three times a week.		

4 Read this itinerary for a four-night holiday in Cairo, Egypt. Then, using the information given, complete part of the personal letter (below) which was written by someone on the holiday. Write the missing words or phrases on a separate piece of paper. The first answer has been given as an example. **Use no more than two words for each space.**

ITINERARY

Thursday Depart in the afternoon from London Gatwick by British Airways scheduled flight to Cairo. Transfer included to your selected hotel (Cosmopolitan, Inter-Continental or Marriott).

Friday After breakfast at your hotel, depart for a full day excursion visiting the Pyramids and Sphinx in the morning, and Memphis and Sakkara complex in the afternoon.

Saturday After breakfast depart for a morning visit to the Egyptian Museum continuing to the Khan El Khalili Bazaar in the afternoon.

Sunday After breakfast at your hotel depart for a tour of Salak El Din Citadel and Sultan Husslin Mosque. Afternoon free.

Monday Transfer to Cairo Airport for your morning departure by British Airways to London Gatwick or extend your stay in Cairo by one or more days.

Dear Lisa, Cairo, Sunday afternoon

Was it only three days ago that we (49) .took off. from Gatwick? We seem to have done so much! We (50) .... at Cairo Airport after an excellent flight, and were (51) .... to the hotel which we (52) ...., the Inter-Continental. After a good night's sleep, we got up, (53) ...., and were picked up by coach from the hotel to (54) .... a full-day excursion.

In (55) .... we visited the Pyramids and the Sphinx, and that (56) .... in the afternoon by a tour of Memphis and Sakkara. All fascinating, but I found it (57) ...., which is why I'm having a quiet hour in my hotel room.

Yesterday was another tiring day, too. We (58) .... the morning touring the Egyptian Museum, and then wandered the Khan El Khalil Bazaar, where I bought a (59) .... I'm sure I paid (60) .... for them, but I don't care. They'll always (61) .... of this fabulous trip!

Since I've been here I (62) .... lots of photos which you can see when I get home. They might (63) .... to come on this trip: it really is an experience.

Section C

5 Choose the best phrase or sentence (given opposite) to fill each of the blanks in the following text. Write one letter **(A-J)** in each of the numbered spaces.

NOTE: Five of the suggested answers do not fit at all.

AVALANCHE!

IF YOU'RE CAUGHT IN AN AVALANCHE of any significant size, the chances of being buried are almost certain. After just 30 minutes of burial, your chances of survival drop to 50 per cent. After three hours of burial, there is only a ten-per-cent chance you are still alive. In terms of depth, if you're buried deeper than one metre, (64) .... If you're buried deeper than two metres, you're out of luck — you cannot dig yourself out, you're too deep for companions to find you, and (65) ....

Shockingly, most large avalanches triggered by skiers reach speeds near 120 kmph within seconds after initial release. It's impossible to maintain control travelling that fast on skis.

Large, dry powder-avalanches have been clocked at over 300 kmph. (66) .... , smash cars like pancakes, and rip homes in half. The largest single avalanche disaster in North America was caused by a quick thunderous slide that tore a train off its tracks and killed 96 of the 118 passengers.

The slowest-moving avalanches are the heavy, wet ones — sometimes travelling only ten kmph. Their mass alone causes havoc. In 1982 a wet avalanche began moving on the slopes above the small town of Alta in the Rocky Mountains in the US. (67) ...., then crush it like a miniature doll's house.

Small, wet avalanches can also be dangerous; glissading mountain-climbers often initiate them. The thick goo then sucks the sliding climber into its moving mass, and (68) ...., he may be swept off a cliff or into a boulder-strewn gully.

A at speeds like these, such a massive weight of snow and ice is unstoppable

B the townspeople had time to move to a safe place and watch the avalanche slowly reach the town chapel

C more than likely, the weight of snow will have already crushed you

D unless he is in radio contact with his base camp at the foot of the mountain

E these avalanches will pluck mature trees four feet in diameter from their roots

F all the people could do was watch as their new town hall was hit by the mountain of snow

G you have less than a fifty-fifty chance of coming out alive

H although you may well be a very experienced skier

I if the climber cannot control his descent through ice-axe self-arrest

J it is 100% certain that the average skier would have suffocated by then

6 You recently attended a sports club association meeting as the representative of a small sports club. The meeting was about a forthcoming week's holiday camp open to members of any sports club in the association. While at the meeting, you made these notes.

Summer Holiday Camp — 4-11 Aug. — White Mountain Village

(69) *Numbers limited — 6 places our club — start thinking now*

(70) *Activities: choose from a range — facilities for all sports — tennis, swimming, badminton, etc. + canoeing, walking, climbing, etc.*

(71) *Equipment: all equipment can be provided — any loss or damage to be paid for.*

(72) *Accommodation: called a 'Camp', but live in chalets — beautiful*

(73) *Each chalet — fully furnished — equipped everything necessary — incl. bedding, crockery, cutlery, washing machine.*

(74) *Cost: $250 per adult. Under-18s, $175 — includes everything.*

(75) *Insurance: Must take out insurance — $10 p.wk.p.p.*

(76) *Travel to Camp — make own arrangements — not incl. in cost.*

(77) *Thinking of going — let me know early — make provisional bookings.*

Using the notes, write (on a separate piece of paper) an information handout for any members of your club that might be interested in going to the camp. You must include everything in the notes and must not add any extra ideas of your own. You may add words and change the form of words where necessary.

White Mountain Village: Summer Holiday Camp
4th-11th August

This year the Summer Holiday Camp is to be held in a new venue, the White Mountain Village, which was opened only last year.

(69) *Numbers on the holiday are limited and our club has only been allocated 6 places, so start thinking now.*

(70) ______________________________

(71) ______________________________

(72) ______________________________

(73) ______________________________

(74) ______________________________

(75) ______________________________

(76) ______________________________

(77) ______________________________

Should you need any further information, please don't hesitate to contact me.

PAPER 4 : LISTENING

Time: Approx. 45 minutes

In this test you will hear four extracts of spoken English and you will be given time to choose your answers to the questions or to write answers. Before you listen to each extract, read the questions carefully. Read or look again while you are listening and choose **A, B, C** or **D**, complete the sentences, or do whatever you are asked to do. In **Section A**, **Section C** and **Section D** check your answers while you are listening for the second time. In **Section B** you will only hear the piece once.

Section A

Read the following information and look at questions 1-5. You're going to hear the beginning of a lecture about dinosaurs. For each of the questions 1-5, listen and decide which is the best answer, **A, B, C** or **D**. When you have finished, you'll hear the piece again.

1 The 'Slow, Slow, Quick, Quick, Slow' title of the lecture reflected

A the speed at which the lecturer spoke at different times.
B the different theories about dinosaurs.
C the dances performed by dinosaurs.
D the pace of life in the 19th and 20th cenuries.

2 The lecturer criticised the dictionary definition she quoted because

A it described dinosaurs as long-tailed creatures.
B it did not refer to fossil evidence.
C it suggested they were all massive.
D it referred to them as cold-blooded.

3 What view of dinosaurs did scientists have in the 1890s?

A They were regarded as very active, warm-blooded creatures.
B They were thought to be slow-moving, warm-blooded animals.
C They were seen as slow-moving cold-blooded creatures.
D They were thought of as being cold-blooded, but active animals.

4 How were dinosaur skeletons mounted in museums in the 1890s?

A As if they were flying.
B They were always rearing up on their hind legs.
C Normally just standing.
D Usually in a running or 'dancing' pose.

5 What had happened by the 1960s?

A There had been two changes of theory about dinosaurs.
B Dinosaurs had come to be seen as very slow creatures.
C Scientists had decided that dinosaurs must have been like modern reptiles.
D There had been a complete shift away from the fast-footed view of dinosaurs.

Section B

Read the following information and look at questions 6-15. You've just turned on the television in time to catch the weather forecast for the next 24 hours for a place called Squareland. Study the map and the Key and the incomplete statements 11-15. For questions 6-10 look at the map, listen, and circle the appropriate letter or letters for the weather in that part of the country. For questions 11-15 about the outlook for the weekend, complete the blanks in the statements. Listen very carefully: you will hear the forecast only once.

SQUARELAND

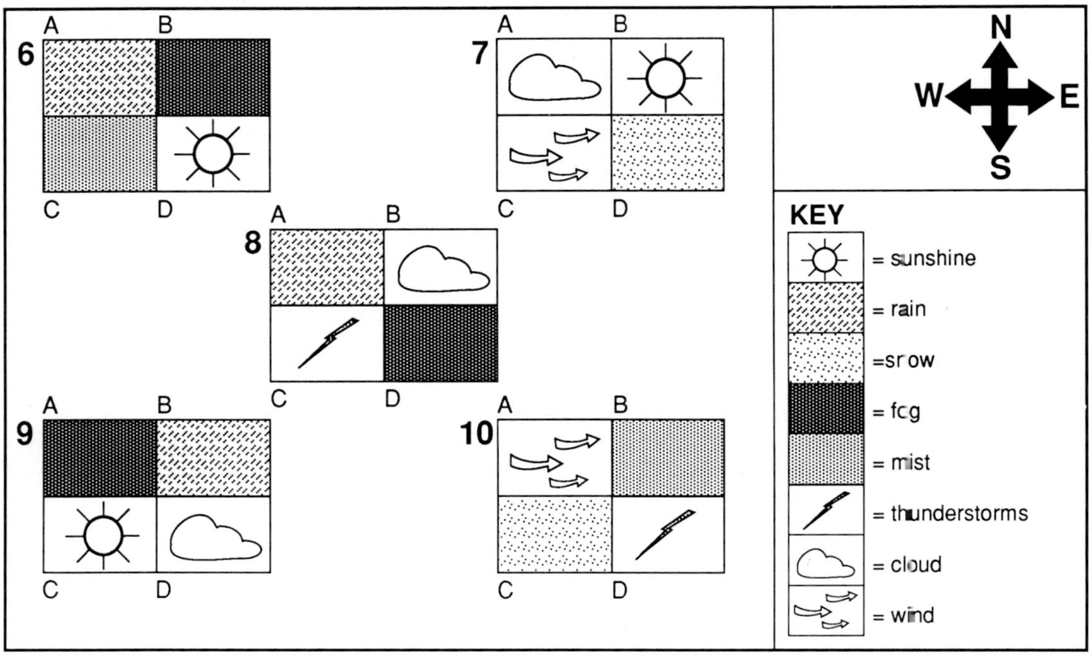

The weekend forecast for the south-east is for (11) ________________ .

The weather in the centre of the country is likely to become (12)________________.

It will turn cloudy and wet in the (13) ______________ of the country.

In the north-east, there will be snow, but it will also be (14) ____________ and

(15) ______________ .

Section C

Read the following information and look at questions 16-25 at the top of page 93. You're going to hear part of a conversation between two English people talking about the holidays they took separately last year. As you listen, answer the questions. Mark your answers by circling **'M'** (for the man), **'W'** (for the woman), or both if appropriate. If neither of them gives any information for you to answer the question, circle **'Neither'**. When you have finished, you'll hear the piece again.

Which of them

did something he or she had always wanted to do?	16	**M**	**W**	**Neither**
went by sea to his or her destination?	17	**M**	**W**	**Neither**
went away on his or her own?	18	**M**	**W**	**Neither**
went to two concerts?	19	**M**	**W**	**Neither**
obviously ate out in restaurants most of the time?	20	**M**	**W**	**Neither**
got worse restaurant service than in England?	21	**M**	**W**	**Neither**
had to go in winter because of work?	22	**M**	**W**	**Neither**
managed to get away from other tourists?	23	**M**	**W**	**Neither**
thought the holiday overall was very cheap?	24	**M**	**W**	**Neither**
was taken ill with food poisoning during the holiday?	25	**M**	**W**	**Neither**

Section D

Questions 26-35. Read the following information and the lettered descriptions below. You're going to hear some views about British TV programmes from letters sent in by ten foreign viewers. Indicate their points of view by putting the appropriate letter (A, B, C, etc.) against the number of the speaker. There are more views than you will hear. When you have finished, you'll hear the piece again.

This viewer ...

26 ... **A** clearly likes programmes that look into the future.

27 ... **B** would like to see less insular news programmes.

28 ... **C** probably gave the producer the idea for this particular programme.

29 ... **D** watches ballet and classical music.

30 ... **E** would like to see worldwide travel programmes.

31 ... **F** only saw part of a programme and wants more information.

32 ... **G** suggests a new series about the English language.

33 ... **H** complains that their country has been ignored.

34 ... **I** would like political review programmes to be less insular.

35 ... **J** can't understand the use of 'Britain' and 'Scotland' in sports programmes.

K would like to see more pop music featured in programmes.

L would like more situation comedy.

PAPER 5 : SPEAKING

Time: Approx. 15 minutes

Work in pairs throughout this Speaking Paper.

Phase A

Even though you might know each other well, do the following:

- Introduce yourself to your partner.
- Tell your partner about how you like to spend your holidays.
- Ask your partner some questions to find out more about the most interesting holiday he or she has ever spent.

Phase B

Student 1: turn to page 99. **Student 2**: turn to page 100.

Do not look at each other's material.

Phase C

Look at the photos opposite and discuss the questions your teacher puts to you.

Phase D [Teacher]

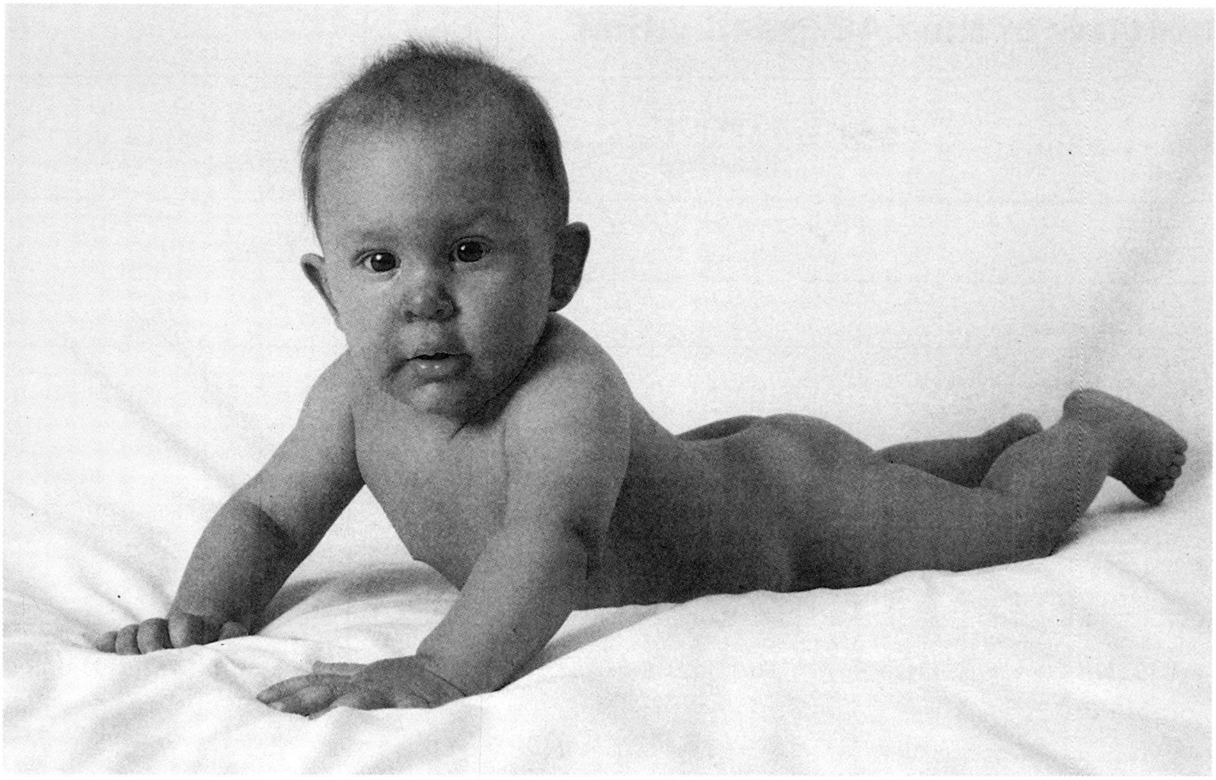

Overview of the CAE Examination

	PAPER 1 **Reading**	PAPER 2 **Writing**
TIME	1 hour	2 hours
% OF MARKS	20%	20%
SECTIONS	4 texts	**A** Compulsory question **B** Choice of topic
OUTLINE OF QUESTIONS	The questions on the texts involve matching and multiple-choice. You will always have to do some skim reading.	**A** You must read something and then write about 250 words based on what you have read. **B** You choose one of four tasks and write about 250 words.

'APER 3 **:nglish in Use**	PAPER 4 **Listening**	PAPER 5 **Speaking**
hour 30 mins.	45 mins.	15 mins.
'0%	20%	20%
Blank-filling: vo questions Correction: wo questions : Text completion: vo questions	**A** Monologue **B** Monologue **C** Two or more speakers **D** Short extracts	**A** **B** **C** **D**
. Two texts with blanks for ou to fill in. With the first ou are given multiple- hoice options to choose 'om. In the first question you ave to correct some iistakes in, for example, rammar or spelling. In the econd you have to change piece of writing from one yle to another e.g. from ormal to informal style. In the first question here ou have a text with a umber of gaps each dicating that a sentence or art of a sentence is missing. here is a list of options nder the text and you ecide which option fits ich of the gaps. the second question you e given some notes which ou must write out in full.	You hear every section twice *except* Section B. In all the sections the questions may ask you to tick boxes, complete plans, label diagrams, choose from multiple-choice options and so on.	**A** You and your partner introduce yourselves to the examiners and vice versa. **B** You each take a turn at looking at a picture of some kind and talking about it for a minute or so. **C** You and your partner discuss and solve a problem of some kind together. **D** The two examiners will talk to you both about some aspect of the speaking test.

EXAM THREE: Paper 5 Speaking — Phase B

Student 2:

1 Look at these photos. Describe each room in as much detail as possible to your partner.

2 Look at the photos on page 72. Discuss which of these people is most likely to live in the four rooms you have photos of. Look at each other's pictures now, too.

EXAM FOUR: Paper 5 Speaking — Phase B

Student 1: Study this photo and be prepared to describe it to your partner. After a minute your partner will describe his or her photo to you.

Before

EXAM ONE: Paper 5 Speaking — Phase B

Student 2: Study this photo and be prepared to describe it to your partner. Your partner will describe his or her photo to you first.

EXAM FOUR: Paper 5 Speaking — Phase B

Student 2: Study this photo and be prepared to describe it to your partner. Your partner will describe his or her photo to you first.